POLITICAL THINKERS

edited by Professor Geraint Parry
University of Manchester

7
ARISTOTLE

POLITICAL THINKERS

ARISTOTLE

John B. Morrall

Senior Lecturer in Political Science
London School of Economics and Political Science

London
GEORGE ALLEN & UNWIN
Boston   Sydney

First published in 1977

ISBN 0 04 320121 0 Hardback
0 04 320122 9 Paperback

Printed in Great Britain in 10 on 11 Point Plantin
by Biddles Ltd, Guildford, Surrey

To
my wife Yvonne,
our sons Philip, Mark, Paul,
David and Andrew
and to my mother and brother

PREFACE

This version of the usual apology for the appearance of a new work on a familiar author might perhaps justifiably point to the relative absence of works in English during this century which aim at presenting the university student as well as the general reader with an overall conspectus of Aristotle's political thought. Compared with the case of Plato, the paucity of such general guidance is striking, and has frequently impressed itself upon the present writer in the course of a number of years of teaching the topic at university level. The last attempt at such a book (and indeed the only English attempt in this century) was made by Ernest Barker in 1908 and a lot of critical and scholarly water has flowed under many academic bridges since then. Even books purporting to provide general surveys of Aristotle's philosophy as a whole tend to give very short measure on his political theory. It would be presumptuous to hope that the present impressionistic sketch can be the magisterial work that is so badly needed in this field, but at least it can try to direct the attention of its presumed readers to what it conceives to be the main points of interest in Aristotle's approach to politics and to venture some evaluation of its contribution to human reflection on life in society.

Some may object to the overlong character of the two background chapters before Aristotle even appears on the scene. The procedure may be mistaken, but it is deliberate and is based on the opinion that Aristotle makes more political sense if his statements are read in the light of some knowledge of how the Greek tradition as a whole viewed political life and the problems arising from it. In particular the author makes no apology for devoting as much space as he could get away with to that great imaginative political thinker, Aeschylus, in the 2500th anniversary celebration of his birth.

The author owes many debts – to his family, his friends, colleagues and pupils, the whole process illustrating the charmed circle of reciprocity and friendship which for Aristotle formed the ideal basis for social life. He wishes to express his gratitude for the forbearance of the editor of the series in which the book appears, Professor Geraint Parry of Glasgow University, and of its publisher, Mr Charles Furth, from both of whom he received constant courtesy and consideration during the rather lengthy gestation of the book. He would wish to thank Dr Fred Rosen of the London School of Economics, and Mr Dale Hall of University College, Swansea, for stimulating help and suggestions which made for enlightenment, while he would also like to pay tribute to the helpfulness which his friend, Mr Geoffrey

Thomas, showed in directing his attention to little-known literature on the subject which might otherwise have been missed, and in many cases making his burden easier by providing him with Xerox copies of it. He would not like either to forget what he has learnt from discussing the subject with pupils at University College, Dublin, and at the London School of Economics. He has learnt much from all.

JOHN B. MORRALL

London School of Economics and Political Science 1976

CONTENTS

'We've got to purge Aristotle from our system.'

'I've never even read him, so why do I have to purge him from my system?'

'It's proof of his grip on Western Man that he dominates the thinking of people who have never heard of him.'

(Conversation piece from Peter de Vries's novel, *Reuben, Reuben*)

> If a Chopper chopped for seven days
> At all within his reach
> He'd not complete his loathsome task
> Of filling up the breach;
> But if he found kind friends to ask
> To help him and to teach
> His work would very soon be done
> And he'd be free to preach.

(From the anonymous epic arranged by 'Mother Vonnis', *The Deeds of Sarper, Marley Scamper, Sweet Beef, Moz and Foolery*)

Chapter I

The Greek Political Dream

This also said Phocylides:
A tiny rock-built citadel
Is finer far, if ordered well,
Than all your frantic Ninevehs.

The lyric epigram by the sixth-century poet Phocylides (here quoted in C. M. Bowra's translation) gives in a succinct artistic moment apt expression to both the complacency and the aspiration which lay as twin elements in the heart of Greek feeling about the *polis*. The sense that this small, beleaguered unit, leading its precarious struggle for existence in the midst of a hostile and unpromising natural environment, was yet the repository of a nobler way of life than that of the autocratic splendours of Near Eastern civilisations, is strikingly obvious; but so is the qualifying demand that to retain this ideal superiority the *polis* must embody certain principles of legitimate order, without which it had no justifiable *raison d'être*. The whole of Greek political thinking revolved round the debate on what these principles exactly were and how they could be best translated into the world of practice.

Many city units had been chronologically prior to the *polis* in the civilised history of the ancient world. What quality was it which gave to the Greeks themselves, and to later historical observers, the conviction that the *polis* possessed an epoch-making uniqueness when compared with these older and often more elaborately articulated urban structures? The element of autonomous individual participation in the life of the *polis* community, greater or less as this participation might be according to the widely varying regimes involved, has been rightly singled out by many scholars as the differentiating factor we are looking for. The other urban units of the ancient world centred on the worship of a divine ruler, the incarnate voice of unchallengeable cosmic forces, as in Egypt, or the steward of basically indifferent or hostile superhuman beings, as in Mesopotamia (whose legendary system depicted Man as owing his very existence to the wish of the gods to create a subordinate Caliban-like being for the performance of disagreeable and degrading chores). The rise and fall of cities was explained in terms of the varying fortunes of the amoral struggles between their respective divine masters. Unity and order within the city was not the product of common acceptance of mutual obligations, but a strictly regimented performance of functions laid down from above by the cosmically appointed hierarchy of priest and king.

In pointing up the contrast between the Greek *polis* and these other ancient urban formations, it would be an exaggeration to deny the existence of a cosmic religious dimension to the Greek universe. The Olympian gods could be in many aspects as incalculably cruel and irrationally unpredictable as their counterparts in the Near East (an area indeed from which many of them seem to have come); from the first, however, the gods of Greek mythology present what might be called a political rather than a cosmic significance as their primary distinguishing feature. Their mutual inter-relations rest on a constantly developing framework of initiative and counter-move, dictated by individual interests and objectives; the doings of the divine protagonists in the *Iliad* and the *Odyssey* may often seem to the modern reader as ancient anticipations of the diplomatic moves and counter-moves of the power politics of recent times. Except for their prerogative of immortality there is indeed little to differentiate the Homeric gods from the human actors in the stories of the epics.

This 'politicising' of the concept of the divine by the archaic Greek imagination was paralleled by the growing tendency to view *human* politics as being primarily conditioned by the interplay of interacting individual *personal* aims and actions rather than by obedience to a rigidly operating cosmic pattern, as was believed by the greater Asiatic civilisations (the more distant Indian and Chinese cultures being as subject to this tendency as the Near Eastern civilised centres).[1] Instead of political life being viewed as a rather diluted mirror of the cosmic order (embodied for the ancient monarchical civilisations for the most part in the system of astronomy and astrology), the Greeks from Homer onwards took the bold step of deducing that politics, cosmic as well as human, could be assessed in terms of *personality*. This new way of looking at social and political behaviour could not be content with describing the external impact of one person's behaviour on another; 'A did this to B with the support of god C' was no longer a sufficient description of a political event. What was needed in addition was an examination in depth of what elements in A's personal compound led him to behave in this way to B and why

14

the divine C should have thought fit to encourage B to behave in the way he did. Questions of what the Greeks, and we after them, were to call 'psychology' and 'ethics' were thus raised as the inescapable subject matter of political inquiry. These conditioning factors of inquiry did not possess the same immutable quality of certitude which a pattern of interpretation by cosmic determinism would carry with it; unpredictability and the idiosyncrasy stemming from the personal quirks of character of unique agents would henceforth have to figure in any convincing account of historical events and political processes.

The first words of Homer's *Iliad* set the tone for this distinctive type of social investigation. 'The Wrath of Achilles is my theme', declares the poet, 'that fatal wrath which, in fulfilment of the will of Zeus, brought the Achaeans to so much suffering'.[2] Thus the dominance of a particular emotion in a particular human mind is pinpointed as the immediate cause for the harrowing chain of events which the epic is to trace out to its culminating moment when Priam stands before Hector's funeral pyre in a final moment of sorrow which sums up and passes judgement on the long-drawn-out tragedy of the fateful war. We can confine ourselves to Book II for reference to an extended passage which may serve as illustrative of the interweaving of personality and politics which was to become the hallmark of Greek thought on society and those who formed it.

To punish Agamemnon for his unjust treatment of Achilles when the commander-in-chief of the Greek forces had seized Achilles's concubine, Briseis, Zeus decides to mislead Agamemnon into launching an ill-fated attack on the Trojans. A 'false dream' is dispatched to the sleeping Agamemnon to inform him that the Olympians have reached a consensus to support the Greeks against Troy (the consensus has been reached by the eloquence of Zeus's consort Hera, a consistent advocate for the Greeks). Emboldened by this fallacious hope, Agamemnon summons the Assembly of the Greek forces, a kind of soldiers' parliament which already serves as a political forum.[3] Before addressing the Assembly, Agamemnon speaks to the smaller body of chieftains who comprise the royal Council. It is significant that we are here presented, before the *polis* in its developed form has even taken shape, with the familiar Greek political triad of executive, council and assembly, which even democratic Athens would accept as axiomatic. Agamemnon lets the leaders into the secret of his stratagem – for the purpose of carrying the Assembly with him, he proposed to argue for an abandonment of the siege, the opposite of his real wishes. He counts on a patriotic backlash by the troops which will whip up enthusiasm for the frontal offensive which is his own objective. The troops however accept his arguments all too readily and begin to stream off towards the ships in a disorderly evacuation. The rot is only stopped by the intervention of Hera and Athene, the inveterately anti-Trojan goddesses, the latter of whom descends into the middle of the fleeing soldiers and instructs Odysseus (the archetype for Homer of human cleverness and 'know-how') to check the stampede. 'Deal with them man by man'[4] Hera has advised Athene; the two goddesses are aware that the individual psychology of the humblest soldier is a considerable factor in the overall political situation. In the same spirit Odysseus goes here and there among the troops, persuading (in the case of the nobles) or threatening (a technique reserved for commoners) as was necessary. Odysseus's arguments may be monarchist-sounding ('We cannot all be kings here: and mob rule is a bad thing. Let there be one commander only, one King, set over us by Zeus'),[5] even smacking of Divine Right; but there is no escaping the fact that he cannot count on unquestioning obedience from the troops in the same way as a Babylonian or Assyrian or Persian monarch could have done; exercise of leadership over these early Greek soldiers already necessitates entering into an elementary political dialogue with them, a dialogue which takes account to some extent of the motivating forces ruling their status and personality. Consent has to be obtained; it cannot be taken for granted, even if the persuasion tactics used may only be thinly disguised shows of force.

Consensus and agreement based primarily on persuasion and conviction is then already present in the Homeric picture of society, and these qualities provide in large measure a substitute for the deterministic cosmic systems which the older Asiatic civilisations had used as their pattern for social order. Hesiod (c. 700 BC), slightly later than Homer, approaches the problem of order from a different but complementary angle. From him we do not hear of consensus and personal agreement: indeed (in the fable of the Hawk and the Nightingale) he seems to scout their very possibility; politics is a question of the application of power and it is futile to deny this. What matters is the manner in which the power is used. Hesiod's fable is intended to appeal to the conscience of rulers (there is no other practical check upon them) to frame their government according to justice. Justice for Hesiod is the foundation-stone of social order. He personifies it as the daughter of Zeus, who complains to her father

> Of the unjust hearts of men,
> Until the city suffers for its lords
> Who recklessly, with mischief in their minds,
> Pervert their judgements crookedly . . . [6]

16

Hesiod's *Dike* embodies an exalted moral conception of right behaviour; but it is lacking in the sense of consciously reciprocal obligation between differing classes and individuals which is a feature of Homer's outlook. To that extent Hesiod's ethic of justice in society is paradoxically more exclusively aristocratic than Homer's. His concept of *Dike* is not a plea for genuine harmonious collaboration between different sections of the community; it does not challenge the right of the landed aristocratic elite to enjoy a monopoly of power; indeed it accepts as natural that the *polis* (the word is beginning to be used by Hesiod in its classical sense) should prosper or suffer as a direct result of the aristocracy's actions. Hope for positive improvement is rested solely on the possibility that the 'lords' may see the light provided by *Dike* and may live by that light of justice in their dealings with the subordinate members of the community.

This paternalistic ethic was not to be that which was to gain ground in the development of the *polis* from its original connotation of protective inner fortress towards its later meaning of comprehensive urban community and even of supreme cultural unit, achieved or only (as with Plato and others) dreamed about. New techniques of communal warfare, new economic standards derived from mercantile expansion and the large-scale use of coinage as primary means of exchange, shattered the aristocratic political monopoly and opened the way to uncharted political roads. 'The city is pregnant' moaned Theognis (sixth century), a displaced aristocrat, 'and I fear she'll bear a violent leader of civil war; the people still have sense, but those in charge are turning, stumbling into evil ways.'[7] The rampant individualism expressed by the more colourful of the lyric poets such as Archilochus and Sappho is met by Theognis by a call for moderation in almost Aristotelean terms:

> Walk calmly as I do, the middle road;
> Don't give to this man, Kurnos, that man's goods.[8]

or:

> Not too much zeal! The middle way is best;
> There, Kurnos, you'll find good, so hard to get.[9]

The revolutionary social upheaval which can be sensed beneath the lapidary epigrams of the sixth-century poets made it inevitable that if Hesiod's concept of justice was to survive it had to break its paternalistic moorings and link itself with a revised version of the Homeric picture of ordered effort through communal co-operation. In

17

the event it was in Athens, with its unique twofold character as ancient Mycenaean centre and yet also as the epitome of the commercial and trading spirit of the new age, that a number of attempts were made over the 250 years between *c.* 600 and 350 BC to link ordered justice with the consent of the governed.

Our literary mirror-image of the first Athenian answer to this fundamental problem of politics comes from a figure central in the practical implementation of the solution – Solon himself (born *c.* 640), ancestor of Plato, and hailed by all later Athenians of all shades of opinion as the ancestor of their city's constitution and political tradition. Much about Solon's authority and reforming activity still remains unclear, and would be still more obscure if we did not possess invaluable fragments of the lyric poetry in which he himself stated his aims and estimated how far he had succeeded in realising them. It does seem certain, however, that about 590 Solon was given power of an almost dictatorial character over the Athenian *polis* for the purpose of settling the chronic economic inequalities resulting from the impact of the new moneyed economy on the traditional agricultural order. Solon did so by declaring a cancellation of all existing debts and a forbidding of slavery of the person in payment for future debts; and he followed up these economic measures by giving the lower classes for the first time a share in the judicial activity of the city. These measures, though based, like Hesiod's pleas for social justice, on the feeling that political and economic rights were ultimately moral issues, went beyond the earlier poet's horizon by making the commoners themselves participate in administering the laws by which they were to be governed. Solon justified this apparently radical break with tradition by arguing that his solution alone would guarantee the spontaneous harmony and order which would provide the co-operative unity of all the rival interests in the city, and would bring an end to the over-riding conflict between rich and poor. Solon had no intention of creating an egalitarian society by abolishing wealth and privilege; instead he felt that he was acting as a true conservative by placing the traditional order on a more stable basis. Nevertheless he was in fact opening up a new path in political order for both Athens and Greece. His slogan of *eunomia* (government in ordered harmony by consensus between classes and interest groups) became a keyword which was to symbolise a *polis* in which unity and peace prevailed because every party felt that they could freely join in achieving a common purpose for the benefit of all and each.

Solon's gospel of *eunomia* is remarkable by reason of its frank espousal of the principle of communal solidarity implemented by a curbing of the unlimited egoistic assertion of individual *arete* ('excellence' in proving oneself stronger in a given field that one's competitors).[10] Solon's outlook is all the more striking because of the strong evidence that he himself felt the pull towards the realisation of his individual drives to self-assertion and self-gratification as strongly as any and perhaps more strongly than most. If his writings do at times strike a prophetic note, he is a prophet more at home in a background of roses, wine and women than of the desert; one of his poetic fragments boasts of his capacity, even in older age, to engage in active sexual enjoyment. He was also aware of the more serious political temptation to make use of his position as mediator and arbiter in the civic conflicts of his city to make himself the autocratic master of Athens. His historic decision to forgo the prize and retire into life as a private citizen is expressed in words which are themselves, somewhat paradoxically, an expression of the nobler elements of which the egoistic ideal of *arete* was itself capable:

If I have spared my fatherland, if I have not turned my hand to tyranny and brutal force, if I have not soiled and stained the character I had before, I am not ashamed, but rather think, by acting as I have, I rise above all other men.[11]

The same personal self-confidence shows itself in other verses in which Solon, looking back after his days of power are over, presents his own apologia to apparent critics:

Power as much as sufficient I placed in the hands of the people;
Nothing I took from their rights; nothing I added to them.
Likewise for those who were mighty, whom men esteemed for their riches,
I contrived that they should have nothing but what was seemly.
There I stood with my shield protecting the one and the other.
Neither this party nor that did I allow to win wrongly.[12]

In another poem Solon indicates the source of his strength:

. . . This is what I did
By power of the law, combining force and right
In one, and so encompassed all my promises.
My laws I wrote for all, for high and low alike,
And dealt an evenhanded justice out to each.[13]

Hesiod's seemingly impossible dream had, even if only momentarily, come true. Forces and justice had become allies. The *tour de force* had been achieved primarily by the right ordering of the personality of the ruling statesman, an ethical self-mastery which in turn enabled the statesman to equip the *polis* with the means to order itself in freedom. This essential connection between the governing factors in personality and those in politics was always to be regarded as fundamental by Greek thought. As far back as Homer we have seen that consideration of the characteristics of personality were viewed as integral parts of any truly political process.

The establishment of democracy in Athens in the fifth century BC was an institutional expression of this conviction. By 460 all adult male native citizens were entitled to vote in the Assembly and be appointed to any official post in the *polis,* and the stripping of the last political privilege from the Areopagus, the Athenian 'House of Lords', the last bastion of the hereditary aristocracy, marked the final triumph of the Commons. It had been an age of revolution and upheaval and the more thoughtful adherents of the new democracy were anxious to remove the suspicion that *demokratia* was a veiled tyranny by numerical force. Aeschylus the dramatist, himself a veteran of the battle for freedom against the Persians at Marathon and Salamis, devoted much of his dramatic output (of which only a lamentably small fraction survives) to the problem of reconciling change with order and justice with freedom.

In essence Aeschylus's answer is the same as that of Solon, but with greater understanding and exploration of the part played by personality in determining the course of society, both cosmic and human. Solon is by no means unaware of the divine dimension but, like Hesiod, he adopts a rather simplistic approach in interpreting divine dealings with Man. Zeus is associated by Solon with the rigid causality of crime and punishment, virtue and reward, in which the founding father of Athenian constitutionalism found the meaning of life and history. Aeschylus finds it impossible to sum up right and wrong in either individual or communal behaviour in these deceptively clear-cut terms. Instead he shows himself intensely aware of the painful division of motivation and intention within the human personality, the political community and even the cosmic principle of divinity itself. All his dramas thus move on three planes of investigation and explanation. *The Suppliant Maidens* hovers on the brink of a possible conflict between the Zeus-inspired instinct of hospitality towards fugitive strangers and the sovereign irresponsibility of popular government. *Prometheus Bound*, most enigmatic of all Aeschylus's plays (though it would probably be less so if we had the rest of the trilogy of which it forms a part), depicts Prometheus, the disinterested benefactor of Man, being tortured and imprisoned by the reigning divinity, Zeus himself, for that very act of kindly benefaction. Zeus has attained his own power by overthrow of his father Kronos and in turn is threatened himself by future overthrow by a rival offspring whom only Prometheus can foresee. The subsequent action of the trilogy[14] would presumably have depicted how, and on what terms, Prometheus reached reconciliation with Zeus and so provided the latter with the information necessary for survival. But, even taking *Prometheus Bound*, as we are forced to do, in isolation, it is plain that Aeschylus sees even cosmic harmony as reachable through tension, confrontation and suffering.

In the *Oresteia*, the only completely surviving Aeschylean trilogy, Aeschylus provides us with a longer view. Behind the harrowing family tragedy of the royal house of Agamemnon we see a cosmic conflict between older and newer divinities. Agamemnon, in the play of that name, returns from Troy and is murdered by his wife, Clytemnestra, and her lover Aegisthus. Agamemnon is avenged in the second play of the trilogy, *The Libation Bearers*, by his son Orestes, who returns from exile and murders not only Aegisthus but even his own mother Clytemnestra. For this matricide he is pursued by the Furies, the demonic avengers of unnatural crimes. The final play, *The Eumenides*, brings to a head the agonising problem of the split within human and divine justice themselves. The simplistic views of retributive punishment presented by Hesiod and Solon are shown to be no longer adequate. The duty of Orestes, laid on him by Apollo, to avenge his father Agamemnon, has led him to commit matricide, which it is the cosmic duty of the Furies to punish. Each side feels it has justice on its side and the culminating scene of the play sees Orestes, supported by Apollo, confronting the Furies before the Areopagus Court at Athens, which is to decide the matter (a graceful compliment by Aeschylus to the old court so recently deprived of all its judicial powers except precisely the right to judge cases of homicide). After an equally balanced debate, the voting of the jurors results in a tie, and the deadlock is only resolved by the decision of Athena, the patron goddess of Athens, in favour of an absolution of Orestes from the guilt which he has incurred. But this is not the end of the matter. Orestes may have been acquitted; but final harmony cannot be reached until Athena has persuaded the Furies themselves to a voluntary acceptance of the verdict. Their acquiescence is recompensed by a change of their own nature concomitant with taking up permanent residence on Athenian soil. The Furies become 'the Eumenides', or 'kindly goddesses'.

Forgiveness rather than strict insistence on justice, harmony based on reconciliation rather than the inflexible application of a legal code, however justified, is presented by Aeschylus as the ultimate solution

21

to the problem of cosmic and human conflict. The old soldier of Marathon, who had managed in *The Persians* to present even the Asiatic foes of Athens in not entirely unsympathetic guise, does not believe in an outright conflict between Good and Evil. For him the real tragedy, in cosmos, *polis* and personality, is the conflict between differing aspects of Good, whose apparent discrepancy can only be resolved by their voluntary and complementary merging in a more adequately comprehensive synthesis. Aeschylus clearly envisioned his own Athenian democracy as possessing the faculty of translating this ideal into political terms. The *Oresteia* is his supreme plea to Athens to provide itself with the will to make this breath-taking vision take on life. Aeschylus's ideal was the imaginative culmination of the Greek political dream. It was no accident that the only genuinely tragic dream known to the ancient world arose in a democratic political structure, and declined with the decay of the society which gave it birth. Tragedy, as the great Attic dramatists saw it, was no clash between black and white, undiluted good and unmitigated evil. It was rather, as Aeschylus already makes clear, a heart-rending confrontation between two modes of good; its resolution is achieved not by the exclusive triumph of one party to the conflict, but by a mutual consensus which does justice to the true claims of both. Reconciliation rather than condemnation is the final keynote.

To put it in other (Aristotelean) terms, the process is one of *catharsis,* the purging of the emotions of fear and pity, not from the spectators (as many misleading interpretations of the *Poetics* have suggested) but from the tragic situation itself. By a supreme paradox the ultimate meaning of Greek tragedy lies in a serene and final optimism. The great tragic characters of Aeschylus and Sophocles are not really either heroes or villains; they are men and women who through their reactions, interior and exterior, to the problems which beset them, exemplify, often unconsciously, the many-sidedness of the universe and of humanity in particular, and point to the comprehension of this many-sidedness by progression through the conflict it engenders to a final reconciling peace. From this point of view, tragedy is strangely less depressing than comedy in its ultimate impact; Aristophanes, the chief comic representative here, is more often than not too prone to rest content with the lampooning of abuses and unpleasant characters by way of brilliant satire, which often becomes caricature (as is obviously the case with his presentation of Socrates in *The Clouds*). Exclusion, rather than comprehension, becomes here the ultimate aim; evil is to be identified by satire, pilloried unmercifully and so destroyed. The result is often brilliantly funny; but after Socrates and Euripides have been thus dismissed, what then? One is left with growing suspicion that, funny as he has been, Aristophanes has missed many of their points, and those perhaps the most important ones. One leaves the comic theatre only half-satisfied. The *Lysistrata* is the only Aristophanic comedy where this criticism is not applicable and perhaps this, as well as its uproariously frank depiction of sexual *mores*, is what has made it appeal particularly to modern audiences. In the *Lysistrata* no one permanently loses from the temporary sexual strike by which the wives of Athens bring pressure to end the war with Sparta; the phallic reunions which ensue when Lysistrata and her comrades have triumphantly carried their point are an image of a deeper union of minds and hearts between cities and sexes in which Aristophanes for once reaches, without self-consciousness, the sublime.

But neither tragedy nor comedy could, I suggest, have existed in its highest form outside the Athenian democratic milieu of the fifth century. This is because tragedy in the Greek sense, which we have attempted inadequately to define, needed a social atmosphere in which the ultimate tensions of individual and society could be perceived and, more important, debated in an atmosphere of intellectual freedom, where even the most outlandish viewpoint could be given a careful hearing. This was the ultimate message of the *Eumenides*. Aeschylus sees Athenian democracy, as it had sprung into existence in his own lifetime (during which he had fought for it twice at Marathon and Salamis), as embodying the best chance for human beings to attain the harmony which he feels lies behind all the struggle and suffering of the cosmic process. 'Knowledge through suffering': this pregnant line from Aeschylus epitomises the Greek feeling that the trouble with Man is not that he lacks goodwill but that he does not know how to implement its demands, how to define priorities in a conflict between 'goods'. The democratic consensus which is symbolically presented in the denouement of the *Oresteia* trilogy, is for Aeschylus to be the social earthly embodiment of the cosmic harmony of which he dreams.

Aeschylus was fortunate enough to die before seeing the beginnings of the collapse of his dream of Athens. Why did Athenian democracy collapse, when there were so many political, economic and cultural factors apparently in its favour? An important part of the answer may well be that Athenian democracy was illogical in not being democratic enough. Its exclusion of 50 per cent or more of its total population (women, slaves, resident foreigners) from the benefits of citizenship (slaves oddly enough being the only one of these categories with even an outside chance of being able by manumission to cross the boundary into the Athenian 'free world') was a standing contradiction of its own premises of equality and freedom.

Another limiting factor was the particularistic and fierce local loyalty which was the fatal legacy of the whole *polis* concept. Like every other Greek city Athens was selfishly jealous of its own interests; even when in possession of its empire in the middle and later fifth century, it proved itself considerably more unimaginative than Rome in missing a golden chance to widen the *polis* horizons by welcoming subject allies into citizenship. Pericles's famous eulogy of his city in the Funeral Oration as reported by Thucydides is a moving declaration of the capacity of the ordinary citizen to share in political responsibility, but the speech contains also encouragement to Athens to persist in the fateful and finally suicidal path of imperialistic expansion. The pages of Thucydides's history of the wartime struggle reflect a growing debasement of the moral currency to suit the needs of a *Realpolitik* more suited to a tyranny than a democracy based on the Aeschylean ideal of consensus. The needs of the state authority were exalted over any other competing loyalty; Sophocles's *Antigone* provides the most telling example of the tragic dilemma to which this could give rise. Whether or not Sophocles is levelling a deliberate criticism in his portrait of Creon at Pericles himself,[15] it remains true that the enunciation of allegiance to 'the unwritten laws' by which Antigone justifies her burial of her brother in defiance of the state law is a recognition by Sophocles that the days when Aeschylus could see as natural and inevitable an alliance between the *polis* and justice were now in the past.

A point of continuity with the older tradition which Sophocles still preserves, however, is the emphasis on the intimate link between personal behaviour and community problems. In *Oedipus Rex*, Thebes is visited by the plague in punishment for Oedipus's unconscious violation of the natural laws condemning patricide and incest. The situation of Oedipus is a strange reversal of the predicament in which Aeschylus placed Orestes; but in the Sophoclean universe, grimmer ultimately than the Aeschylean, pardon for the sinner and harmony for the social fabric (though significantly that of Athens rather than Thebes itself) occurs as a result of the condemnation and complete though voluntary submission of Oedipus rather than in a consensus of freely harmonised interests. In Sophocles the tragic universe created by Aeschylus is beginning to burst at the seams – a parallel and contemporary process to the disintegration of the spirit of Athenian democracy, where consensus was being replaced by naked majority rule. The process reached its *reductio ad absurdum* with the execution of Socrates in 399 in the name of democracy for alleged challenge to religious and ethical traditional city standards.

The viciousness of the anti-Socratic reaction had already been foreshadowed in 424 by Aristophanes's lampoon in *The Clouds*, with its anti-intellectual tone of ridicule of the 'thinking-shop' of philosophy. Euripides's plays provide an illustration in depth of the intellectual and political chaos of the last decades of the century. Most of his plays concentrate on personal issues of conduct and psychology and, though the link-up with a social context is never completely lost, Euripides is clearly an appreciable step farther away from the Aeschylean synthesis than had been Sophocles. His last and probably greatest play, *The Bacchae*, deals with the same problem of divine authority and human rebellion as had provided the chief theme for *Prometheus*. Euripides's play, however, presents the conflict on a consistently lower level, in which a mercilessly unconquerable deity clashes with a rigidly rationalist secular ruler in a polarised fight to a finish which tears to pieces any approximation to a commonly shared universal order, and provides mankind with the stark alternatives of death or brainwashed submission to an irresistable tyrant. The interpretation of life behind *The Bacchae* allows no scope for the optimistic hope of final universal reconciliation held out by Aeschylus.

The fourth century saw the democratic ideal in gradual retreat, though it survived as a constitutional form at Athens for most of the century and beyond. Orators like Aeschines and Demosthenes embody the day-to-day thinking of the ordinary man[16] but this is still linked with traditional stances which would hardly lend themselves to innovative elaboration. In particular the *polis* remained the by now constricting horizon of thought and feeling, modified at best by the pan-Hellenic, anti-Persian propaganda of Isocrates and the plea for ending or at least humanising inter-*polis* warfare by Plato in his *Republic*. These minimal theories were largely ignored in practice and fourth-century political Greek history becomes a dreary record of inter-city war to the knife, with extermination as the penalty of defeat.

The Greek political dream, created by the imagination of the statesmen and poets, was fading. Could the more systematic gaze of philosophy retrieve what had been lost?

Notes Chapter I

1 One must single out the exclusion of ancient Israel from this general statement, due to the presence of unique factors (on any showing) which do not concern the line of argument taken here.

2 Iliad, I (translation by E. V. Rieu, Penguin Classics, 1950, p. 2).

3 It also conferred a certain amount of prestige on those who could

competently play their part in it.
4 *Iliad,* II (Rieu, p. 44).
5 *Iliad,* II (ibid., p. 45).
6 *Works and Days* (translation by D. Wender, Penguin Classics, 1973, p. 67).
7 *Elegies,* 1081–2 b (translation by D. Wender, op. cit., p. 135).
8 ibid., 331–2, p. 108.
9 ibid.
10 By Solon's time *arete* was already beginning to take on its later meaning of 'ethical virtue', but the older meaning, exemplified in the Homeric writings, never lost its appeal for the Greek mind (see the various works of A. W. H. Adkins for detailed discussions of this subject).
11 Fragment 23.8 (translation by H. Fränkel, *Early Greek Poetry and Philosophy,* Oxford, 1975, p. 224).
12 Fragment 5 (ibid., p. 225).
13 Fragment 24 (ibid., p. 226).
14 Of which some fragments (from *Prometheus Unbound*) have survived.
15 As V. Ehrenberg, *Sophocles and Pericles* (Oxford, 1953) suggests.
16 See K. G. Dover, *Greek Morality in the Time of Plato and Aristotle* (Oxford, 1975).

Chapter II

Philosophy
and the *Polis*

Dante in his *Divine Comedy* places Aristotle in a privileged circle in Hell, surrounded by 'his philosophical family', among whom even Plato is included. Dante's elevation of Aristotle to philosophical pre-eminence as 'il maestro di color che sanno'[1] was in line with medieval scholastic tradition, for whom Aristotle was 'The Philosopher' without need for further qualification. This quasi-canonisation of Aristotle as supreme rational authority was not shared by antiquity, for which Aristoteleanism was merely one contestant, though an impressive contestant, for the philosophical palm. Stoicism, Platonism and Epicureanism were three other major rivals with whom Aristotle's 'Peripatetic' school at first competed and was eventually conflated by the synthesising tendency of the later Graeco-Roman world.

Placing Aristotle in this perspective of future centuries may not be too irrelevant, as it gives an accurate illustration of Aristotle's own attitude to previous philosophy, which is usually depicted in his works as providing inadequate answers to questions which his own philosophy professes to solve more correctly. Aristotle has been frequently criticised by modern scholars as having committed the anachronism of placing earlier thinkers in the Procrustean bed of his own formulation of philosophical problems. Aristotle's method may not be the best way to form a genuine historical understanding of previous philosophies, but at the same time it does seem to have been the first sustained attempt to assess the march of philosophy as a sustained pursuit of truth over a long period of historical time, and we are inevitably dependent on it for much of our knowledge of the earlier 'Pre-Socratic' period. The Aristotelean presentation here, as in so many other fields of knowledge, serves to epitomise and in some ways to consummate the spirit actuating past Greek tradition.

This tradition, as far as the philosophical past was concerned, is characterised by a profound dichotomy between two basic ways of interpreting ultimate reality. Both approaches combine a common

27

assumption that human reason can provide its own picture of what really exists or happens beneath the superficial appearance of passing phenomena. The scholars of the more recent decades of our century have not been so insistent as those of the past that Greek rationalism was an absolutely innovative and original departure in the story of the human mind. A number of recent approaches stress the continuity of Greek philosophy with mythological and religious ways of interpreting the world.[2] Aristotle himself is quite aware of the element of truth in this view; in Book A of his *Metaphysics* he deduces that 'Philosophy arose then, as it arises still, from wonder . . . it is for this reason that the lover of myths is in some sense a philosopher, for myth is composed of marvels'.[3] The Greek spirit had in fact always felt the need to obtain a rationally systematic picture of the world of experience. In Homer, the man of reason such as Odysseus is strongly praised, while in the great tragedies there is an element almost of detective work in the desire to find a satisfying explanation for the predicaments in which their heroes are involved.[4]

There is thus no initially abrupt contrast between philosophical and non-philosophical types of Greek thought; it is at first sight difficult to make a distinction, for instance, between Homer's idea of Ocean as the origin of all things[5] and the notion attributed by Aristotle to Thales, the first major Greek philosopher, that everything originated from water.[6] Perhaps the chief distinguishing mark of the early philosophers from their literary contemporaries (such as Aeschylus) was their wish to seek one single impersonal cause or origin of universal phenomena rather than to regard universal order as an interplay of differing, sometimes conflicting but ultimately complementary personal forces, divine and human. W. Jaeger has described 'the growth of Greek philosophy as the process by which the original religious conception of the universe, the conception of the myth, was increasingly rationalised'.[7] We might add that the process reaches its culmination in Plato, where the myth is placed completely in the service of the rational philosophical argument by being used to illustrate it.

The tendency of the early sixth-century philosophers previous to Heraclitus to construct systems resembling the pre-philosophical 'theogonies' (the systematic rearrangement of myths, as by Hesiod, to illustrate the origin of the various generations of gods and men) may very well owe considerable debts to mythological symbolism from the Near East and perhaps even farther afield, though the extent of such influence is as yet difficult to determine. The attempt to ascribe the origin of life to a single impersonal factor (water in the case of Thales, 'the Unlimited' with Anaximander, air with Anaximenes, fire with Heraclitus) is certainly reminiscent of the Near Eastern creation myths, and taken by itself, carries with it implications for ethical and political behaviour which stand in sharp contrast to the world outlook of the poets, tragedians and the politicians of democracy. As we have seen in the paradigmatic example of Aeschylus, this more poetic and imaginative tradition reaching back to Homer emphasised the tensions and conflicts in the cosmic and human order as arising from confrontations between fragmented and complementary differing aspects of goodness, expressed through different personalities. Resolution of the struggle was achieved, as was shown most clearly in Aeschylus's great trilogy, by reconciliation and harmony between the forces concerned, each in themselves good, although incomplete. We have already suggested that this view of life would both encourage a democratic political atmosphere of discussion and would be in turn promoted by it. The monistic view of the early philosophers would, on the other hand, ultimately favour a political outlook more akin to that of the Near Eastern absolutist structures. It might be no accident that the first Pre-Socratics came exclusively from Ionia, always susceptible to Oriental contacts through its position on the Anatolian coastline and from the second half of the sixth century under Persian political control.

At the same time the presence of a strand of pluralist speculation in early philosophy should be noted, as it qualified considerably the dominant monistic trend. The one probably genuine fragment which we have from Anaximander (via the Neoplatonist compiler Simplicius) talks of existing phenomena as passing out of existence 'according to necessity; for they pay penalty and retribution to each other for their injustice according to the assessment of Time'.[8] This obscure and often discussed passage, whatever one's detailed interpretation of it may be, certainly gives the overall impression of speaking in terms of cosmic interaction and reciprocal contact on an almost legalistic basis. It seems probable however that Anaximander thought of the substratum of the universe, his 'Unlimited', as being ultimately a monistic unity into which the plural phenomena of the material universe fade and out of which they cyclically re-emerge. There is a certain movement here and a certain process; but the process is finally subordinate and is swallowed up in the structural monism of the *whole*. There is no trace of Aeschylus's optimism (which we take to be a distinguishing mark of the 'poetic' tradition) about the permanent relevance of the limited and imperfect, but still necessary and complementary *parts* of the universal structure. Nor have we the conviction of the poets, of which Aeschylus once more provides classic expression, that Time itself is not merely a swallower-up of

29

human actions and aspirations, but that rather it validates them, however slowly and painfully, and gives them their depth and meaning.

The first of the philosophers to show much interest in the purposive, almost historical, interpretation of the process of Man's life is Heraclitus, an enigmatic figure, though obviously a thinker of prophetic status. In contrast to most other Greek philosophers, Heraclitus chose to present his message in the form of terse, obscure epigrams in which symbol and imagery are used to invest his meaning with a powerful imaginative impact. This alone would be sufficient to show his affinities with the poetic as well as the philosophical tradition and in many ways he stands, perhaps more than any other Greek writer up to his own time, as typifying the attempt (all too rare) to end the already looming 'quarrel between poetry and philosophy', to use the famous Platonic phrase. Heraclitus's function as a reconciler of the two traditions, old and new, is obscured by his own polemical bellicosity towards earlier and contemporary representatives of either, as well as to the ignorant mass of 'sleeping' men, the servants of illusory 'common-sense' opinion, for whom Heraclitus has as sound a contempt at Plato was to have later.

Heraclitus's meaning has been subject to much controversy. The suggestion may be made that the main difficulties of interpretation stem from an ambiguity in his thought which is itself due to his straddling of the gulf between the poetic and philosophical traditions. On the one hand, he stands with his fellow Ionian physicists in seeking out one prime element (in his case fire, literally or symbolically interpreted) as the source of universal life. This side of his thinking is in debt to the monist tradition; but it is not the only side. Linked with it is his conviction of the unceasing operation of pluralistic change; this is no mere cyclic repetition but a succession of unrepeatable, hence unique events ('You cannot step twice into the same river, for other waters are continually flowing on').[9] The principal participant in this comic drama is the individual human personality, expressed by Heraclitus in the word *psyche*. 'You would not find the frontiers of the personality, though you explored every one of its roads; it has an unmeasurable meaning.'[10]

This individualism of Heraclitus may be traced in faint outline in its application to politics, though once again there is a real ambiguity. Most of the fragments referring to human society breathe an elitist atmosphere in which the populace is derided and denounced for keeping its most able members jealously out of office. Other sayings, however, speak of the supremacy of law, even of a universal natural law, and one fragment, more than usually enigmatic, speaks of the despised 'sleepers' as 'workers and collaborators in what goes on in the universe'.[11] If Heraclitus can hardly be called a democrat, he does none the less appear to share the view of his contemporary Aeschylus that everyone has some part to play, even if it be an unconscious one, in the universal drama. No wonder that Hegel and Marx in their generations, with their own conviction of the reality of the historical and tragic visions,[12] found a deep affinity with Heraclitus.

The significance of Heraclitus in reconciling (as we suggest) the poetic and philosophical outlooks on life may be symbolised by his use of the concept of *Logos* as the determining force in rational understanding of the universe. *Logos* had originally meant 'the act of speech' as well as 'the process of reasoning, calculating, defining'; Heraclitus seems to have been the first to use it in the sense of 'an underlying organisational principle of the universe',[13] and the association of speech and thought implicit in the word would fit admirably with the suggested significance of his message in combining the poetic and philosophical visions.

The combination between stability and movement which Heraclitus had set out to achieve was brusquely and ruthlessly dissolved by Parmenides, who argued (strangely enough in a poem in traditional Homeric hexameter style) that change was incompatible with correct reasoning, because to admit it would lead to the logically absurd conclusion that being and not-being were the same. Parmenides was not very worried by the problem of reconciling his assertion of the impossibility of change and movement with the apparent deliveries of sensory observation. He merely stated that the latter were illusory, though he did not clearly explain why. His bleakly uncompromising assertion of monism snapped the budding rapprochement between the poetic and philosophical traditions which could have been explored along the line suggested by Heraclitean thought, and the invulnerability of his argument in the current stage of logical technique was to present the whole Greek philosophical tradition with an acute problem which was to plague it for a century. Could there be any rational reconciliation between the concepts of stability and change? The poetic tradition, especially in the work of the great Attic dramatists, had assumed that the search for such a reconciliation was of the deepest importance for an understanding of the character of life itself, and Heraclitus had attempted to steer philosophy along the same path. But if Parmenides was right, the whole search was a waste of time, the pursuit of an answer to a totally imaginary question.

The virtual ascendancy of Parmenides over serious Greek philosophical thinking in the rest of the fifth century had side-effects on political thought which are not usually considered as attentively as they should be. First and foremost, the denial by Parmenides and his school of the reality of change took the stuffing, as it were, out of the whole process of rational deliberation on future community policies, a process which lay at the heart of the newly emerged democracy. We may even suggest that the spectre of Parmenides may have been a prime reason why Greek democracy never in fact did frame a systematic philosophy of its own to set against the well-articulated structure of its more powerful intellectual critics. To find a substitute ideology instead of the more comprehensive philosophy of which it had been deprived by the Parmenidean *impasse*, democracy had to retire to the more dubious area of subjectivist and pragmatist thinking. A second fatal legacy from Parmenides pointed the way.

Parmenides's poem was divided into two sections. The first enunciates the uncompromising rejection of the reality of sense perception which has just been discussed. The second section proposes to accept, for the sake of argument, the premiss that sense perception may be used to construct a cosmological system based on distinction and interplay between separate forces, though Parmenides makes very clear that the whole discussion here is nothing more than a humouring of those who cling to the illusion that ordinary observation can supply reliable information about reality. It is far from clear why Parmenides should have taken the trouble to construct this second section,[14] but what is historically significant about this part of his poem is that it initiated a 'let's pretend' attitude into philosophy which could lead to a pragmatism which shelved any attempt to reason about anything other than immediate practical problems.

It is in this atmosphere of growingly materialistic 'realism' that we can best understand the complex of intellectual personalities and techniques usually described as the 'Sophist' movement. In a profound sense it can be viewed as a backlash, a gesture of despairing common-sense in protest against the inexorably static world-picture which the Parmenidean philosophical orthodoxy sought to impose on the free-wheeling play of reason in political action which had become the Athenian ideal, however far short the latter might fall of Aeschylus's vision. The polarisation between reason and practical activity to which the logic of Parmenides's argument ultimately led created its own response in the relativising by the Sophists of religious and even moral factors in the conduct of the life of Man.

The process could be salutary. The insistence on the observation of visible phenomena and the importance of concentrating on the individual and particular which we can see in the medical writings of the Hippocratic Corpus led to considerable advance in the treatment of disease. From the same Hippocratic school stems an interest in assessing the influence of what we should call environmental factors (climate, geographical and ethnographical features, etc.) on the development of individuals and societies. In the work of Thucydides we find an impressive attempt to apply this methodology on a massive historical scale by describing the pathology of Greek society during the Peloponesian War. As we saw in our first chapter, Thucydides's emphasis on the material factors influencing behaviour during the death struggle of the war illustrates also the growing reliance on non-moral and opportunist calculation on *Realpolitik* lines which would seem to have degraded the democratic cause for which, as Pericles saw it, Athens claimed to fight. With the sure touch of a tragedian as well as an historian, Thucydides charts the self-distortion of the Athenian political mind. The opposite pole to the Funeral Speech is provided by the infamous Melian Dialogue, in which Athens coolly and brutally states its intention as well as capacity to subdue the small neutral island for purely strategic reasons; the delegates from the alleged citadel of popular government and justice are not afraid to rest their case on the undiluted law of force; Nature for them is indeed red in tooth and claw. The halfway house between Pericles and Melos is provided by another dramatically stated incident – the debate in the Athenian Assembly over the hasty vote to butcher or enslave the whole civilian population of the rebel city of Mytilene. In the end the Assembly reverses its decision, but does so under the influence of arguments in favour of clemency which are more utilitarian than humanitarian. It is clear that expediency rather than principle rules Athenian political calculations and Melos eventually produces little surprise to the reader.

How far can we blame Sophist pragmatism for the debasement of the moral currency reflected by Thucydides in historical record, Aristophanes in satiric comedy, Euripides in his pessimistic trans-formation of the tragic vision and Socrates in his search for clarity of thinking? It seems clear from our admittedly sketchy first-hand knowledge of the teaching of leading Sophists that not all would answer to the charge of amoralism. Protagoras, a member of an early generation of Sophist teachers, is treated with some respect by Plato in his dialogue and is credited with attempting to base the grounds for civic obligation on a permanent scheme of ethical values. One cannot think of a plausible reason why Plato should present Prota-goras as more idealistic than he really was, and clearly one has to beware in labelling Protagoras as a sceptic *tout court*. On the other hand, the evidence of the surviving Protagorean fragments does seem to indicate a relativistic outlook which one could say would be, at the best, uninterested in any attempt to build a comprehensive philo-sophical system.

The leading Sophist of the next generation, Gorgias, presents a more undilutedly sceptical image. The Platonic dialogue which is named after him seems determined to point out the political amoralism which results from Gorgias's emphasis on the power of rhetorical persuasion as the fundamental force in human relationships. The authentic surviving writings of Gorgias, which are rather more than we have in the case of Protagoras, seem to bear Plato's picture out. The *jeu d'esprit* in defence of Helen of Troy absolves the famous beauty from responsibility for the Trojan War, but only at the cost of maintaining that the human mind is completely at the mercy of cleverly seductive persuasion rather than objective truth. For some of the time Gorgias appears to be satirising the Parmenidean school, but he simultaneously adopts with relish the 'let's pretend' stance to which Parmenides had subscribed in the second part of his poem.[15]

The fragments of writings of a third Sophist, Antiphon, illustrate another issue which must have been brought into prominence, even if not actually initiated, by the Parmenidean breach between reason and experience. With Antiphon we see 'Nature' deliberately contrasted with social usage and customs of whatever kind and presented as no more than the complex of the urge of the individual towards self-assertion and self-satisfaction. The laws of the *polis* can command no more obedience than can result from their outward enforcement; if such enforcement is impossible, so much the better for the individual, who can pursue his purely egoistic objectives with all the more freedom. The *nomos* ('law')/*physis* ('nature') antithesis receives here its most unabashed statement outside the speeches of the 'amoralist' characters, Callicles and Thrasymachus, of Plato's dialogues.

Plato's Socrates of the *Crito* dialogue might almost be intended as a deliberate opposite to Antiphon's gospel of egotism and defiance of social obligation. Socrates, presented with a way of escape from prison, where he awaits his death sentence, refuses to take it on the ground that he is obliged by his lifelong membership of the Athenian *polis* to bow to its legal decision even when he believes it to be based on erroneous ethical assumptions. The dialogue raises the problem with which Plato was to wrestle in varying forms and with varying degrees of success throughout his entire philosophical career. How could the wholehearted pursuit of truth by the philosopher square with his obligation to be a good and fully active citizen?

To answer this question adequately would require a full-scale survey of the entirety of Plato's thinking. Here one can only mention one salient point to which Plato seems to revert in various guises right up to the end of his life. This was the conviction that, if political justice could be achieved at all in the world of practical experience (and sometimes Plato seems to be on the edge of denying this), it could only be by applying ultimate philosophical truths, when discovered, to the lower world of everyday social life. The world of Forms, to which Plato in his middle period ascribed absolute reality, was as little subject to change as the cosmos of Parmenides. Plato did however admit a certain degree of objective if limited reality to the world of sense and opinion, and to that extent he was able to restore to ethical and political thinking the vitality of which Parmenides had deprived it. Plato's later dialogues, in which logical problems are treated at a more intensive and mature level, were able to suggest that the Parmenidean denial of change had owed much of its force to semantic rather than strictly philosophical argumentation and that the dilemma posed by the older philosopher was not inescapable. The later Plato was in fact moving towards an acceptance of change as a legitimate factor in any explanation of the world order, and Aristotle was to carry forward and expand this rediscovery, which marks something of a return to the Heraclitean tradition.

We may return to consider the *Apology* and the *Crito*, which are among Plato's earliest writings, because they express more concisely than some of the later and more elaborate dialogues (for example, the *Republic*) the problems inherent in the relationship between politics and philosophy. They also lay down the essential conditions by which alone, according to Plato, the philosopher can bring peace and harmony to the *polis*. They may thus serve us as manageable specimens of the Platonic approach to politics which was to provide an important element in Aristotle's own thinking.

Plato was not the only writer to present an 'Apology' for Socrates. We have Xenophon's version also and it seems that quite a number of other writers produced similar 'apologies' in the years following Socrates's execution. We can only guess at their contents and surmise in general that their main objective was to disprove accusations that Socrates had been a disloyal citizen; this is certainly Xenophon's main preoccupation. Plato too is alive to the necessity of disproving the slurs on Socrates's citizenship which had been brought by his accusers and which the condemnation by the majority (albeit small) of jurymen at his trial had appeared to substantiate. Naturally we cannot determine how far the words Plato puts into the mouth of Socrates correspond with historical fact; nor is the issue very important. What matters is the part the dramatic figure of Socrates plays in making concrete Plato's own developing views on the confrontation between philosophical truth and political requirements.

In the *Apology* Socrates urges the indispensable role of the philosopher. He is to act as a gadfly to his city, questioning what hitherto had been customarily unquestioned, teaching the citizens not to rest complacently satisfied with familiar, 'common-sense' assumptions. Socrates depicts himself as spurred on by the Delphic Oracle's description of him as the wisest of men to engage in a pilgrimage round the various classes of Athens – the statesmen, the poets, the craftsmen. All of them, he found, were lacking in wisdom as soon as they overstepped the boundary of their own profession or craft. He himself was superior to all at least in one thing – that he knew his own intellectual limitations. Modesty, the lack of *hubris* as the poetic tradition would have put it, is the hallmark of the philosopher.

The modesty of Socrates is not incompatible with a deep and unwavering sense of mission, a mission to persuade his hearers to care for their souls by using their rational faculties to the best effect; 'the unexamined life is not a life worth living'.[16] The mission of Socrates is defined by the symbolism of his *daimon,* the hidden inner force which prevents him from acting in the wrong way. Positive guidance is *not* provided by the *daimon*; in other words, the function of the philosophic intellect is to be critical, even destructive, rather than systematic. This role of almost detached critic has been responsible for Socrates's deliberate abstention from public life for most of his career, though on two occasions he fulfilled the duties of member of the Council to uphold the right administration of the law. Socrates makes it clear that his chief offence in the eyes of the politicians who have brought him to trial on such specious charges is precisely his insistence on submitting the foundations of behaviour, public and private, to a rational *critique*. This is how he has 'corrupted the youth' and a rollcall of names, including that of Plato himself, forms a kind of charter of Apostolic Succession of those who will take the torch of philosophic witness and unflinching inquiry from the dying hand of Socrates. This philosophic quest, Socrates believes, will be pursued even in the after-life (assuming there is one): 'And best of all, to go on still with the men of that world as with the men of this', Socrates goes on, with perhaps a tinge of humour, 'inquiring and questioning and learning who is wise among them, and who may think he is, but is not. Certainly *there* they will not put one to death for that.'[17] The divine comedy of the Socratic quest is, for the *Apology,* an external quest.

Turning to the *Crito,* we find a Socrates more conciliatory, within the basic principles of his position, towards the *polis* than in the *Apology.* In the latter the main emphasis had been on the malevolence of the city leaders, their fear of the searchlight of philosophical rationality, and their readiness to stick at nothing to suppress the philosophical hero. The situation is presented in uncompromisingly black and white terms. The drama is that of a Passion play rather than of a tragedy in the sense in which we have tried previously to define it,[18] of a harrowing clash between different sincerely held interpretations of what is good. No Aeschylean harmony or synthesis could arise from the spirit of the *Apology*. Behind the figure, compellingly arresting still across the centuries, of the old Socrates, uncompromisingly upholding philosophy in defiance, if need be, of the *polis* itself, stands that of his young creator with his scornful *pronunciamento* of the supremacy of undiluted reason. Almost like Orestes, Plato regards himself as commissioned to avenge the fate of Socrates against his unscrupulous and hateful native city.

> I say to you, you who have killed me, punishment will fall on you immediately after my death, far heavier for you to bear – I call God to witness! – than your punishment of me. . . . Those who will call you to account will be more numerous – I have kept them back till now, and you have not noticed them, – and they will be harder to bear inasmuch as they are younger, and you will be troubled all the more.[19]

With the *Crito* we find a change of emotional atmosphere which demonstrates Plato's astonishingly varied range of dramatic expression, as well as of intellectual stance. The rejection of Crito's plan of escape by Socrates provides Plato with the opportunity of making a less one-sided assessment of the issue which divides Socrates as philosopher from his *polis*. In some respects, admittedly, Socrates is as uncompromising as in the *Apology*. Majority opinion is scouted as not worth intelligent attention; all that matters is the verdict of the intellectual elite. At the same time Socrates argues that the *polis* itself has a genuine case which the philosopher must concede, even if he feels that the city has treated him unjustly. If the philosopher evades the punishment inflicted on him, even for a wrong reason, by the legal authority of the *polis*, he is in his turn inflicting a wrong on the *polis*; and to commit wrong is by definition incompatible with the pursuit of philosophical truth. In a powerful personification of the *polis*, Socrates imagines his beloved Athens as reproaching him for any tendency to seek an escape:

> Tell us, Socrates, what is it you mean to do? Nothing more or less than to otherthrow us, by this attempt of yours – to overthrow the laws and the whole commonwealth so far as in you lies. Do you imagine that a city can stand and not be overthrown, when

the decisions of the judges have no power, when they are made of no effect and destroyed by private persons?[20]

By having stayed in Athens throughout his long life, by having enjoyed its benefits of material sustenance and intellectual culture, by having used it as the interlocutor for his philosophical quest, Socrates had accepted the right of the *polis* to call for his allegiance in obeying its verdict. It is important to remember that the *polis* does *not* assert a right to compel Socrates to change his philosophical convictions; what it *does* maintain is that the philosopher must abide by the *polis's* undisputed power to impose obedience to its laws, for without this obedience the pattern of reason to which the philosopher makes his appeal would itself collapse as the regulating force in social life. 'Who could have a city without laws?'[21]

The argument of *Crito* reveals Plato as treading in the footsteps of Aeschylus by exploring the possibility of harmony rather than confrontation in the relationship between philosophy and the city. The conformity of Socrates to the government, even the unjust government, of the *polis,* marks a break in the circle of confrontation and revenge which casts a shade over the heroism of Socrates in the *Apology.* In the *Crito* Plato urges his beloved character to even more sublime heights; Socrates is now to die, not only as a martyr for philosophy (which he still remains) but also, and more important, as a bridge-builder between the exalted world of abstract truth and the more humdrum, but still precious, world of every day.

Plato did not preserve this 'Aeschylean' stance without variation. Indeed his *corpus* of dialogues through to the *Laws* shows a bewildering oscillation of opinion on this topic. The contrast between the Sun and the Cave, which came into the open in the *Republic,* is present implicitly in other dialogues, and the correct response of the philosopher to this contrast is a matter of perennial concern to Plato. The *Apology* and the *Crito,* with their varying attitudes of rejection and co-operation respectively in discussing the philosopher's relation to the city, form the twin poles between which Plato's thought and feeling swing. In the *Gorgias* the assault of Callicles on any sort of moral value calls forth in Socrates's response a momentary common front between ordinary opinion, which accepts the reality of moral laws, and philosophical wisdom, which alone is capable of defining and therefore of validating goodness. In other parts of this dialogue, however, a more severely elitist attitude comes to the fore. Themes which are to receive later elaboration in the *Republic* (such as the analogy of the ruler with the physician and the ideal of justice as the key to political stability) receive much attention.

Socrates presses the contrast with contemporary Athenian politics, which he accuses of acting without any regard for moral or rational principles. 'We are unaware of a single good politician in our State'[22] is a sweeping enough statement, though it must be granted that Callicles's round attack on philosophy in general had already polarised the discussion. Socrates also asserts,[23] 'In my opinion I am one of the few Athenians (not to say the only one) who has attempted the true art of politics, and the only one alive to put it into practice'. Philosophy in fact *is* the only true politics, Socrates argues in a remarkable 'takeover' bid; he is therefore prepared to accept pointblank persecution by the unphilosophical city, almost with relish; for, as the myth at the end of the dialogue shows, eternal punishment in the next world awaits the wicked politicians. Once again the 'Aeschylean' ideal of harmony has receded in favour of a more uncompromisingly rigorist attitude in which the *polis* as it now stands is sentenced to moral destruction. There is a touch almost of megalomania about Socrates's attitude here. The tension between philosophy and politics here develops into a virtual impasse which, as his later works show, alarmed Plato himself. The dilemma with which the death of Socrates had presented Plato in reaching a comprehensively satisfying definition of the relationship between wisdom and political action persists throughout all the dialogues despite Plato's heroic efforts to reach a solution. In the *Republic* he was clearly under the impression that, if any sense at all could be made of political life, it must be by the handing over of full control to the philosophical expert. The process denies all autonomy in effect to politics, but it also carries almost as many dangers for philosophy itself, which runs the risk of becoming a technology for the achievement of a limited political goal rather than the wholehearted contemplative pursuit of truth. As always, Plato was his own keenest critic; the allegory of the Cave reveals him as ultimately pessimistic about his own recipe for social regeneration and at the end of the vast dialogue he falls back on hopes for personal salvation only.

The *Statesman* and the *Laws* show Plato backtracking to a more moderate position. In the former rule by philosophers is to be indirect rather than directly full-blown, as it had been in the *Republic*; in the *Laws,* which (as has been shown)[24] borrows much from existing Athenian practice, Plato calls in the ordinary citizens and offers a constitution based, not on the infallible wisdom of correct philosophical reasoning, but on a judicious mixture of existing political regimes. But, to crown all, the ghost of the *Republic* walks again at the end of the *Laws* with the Nocturnal Council of elder statesmen who are to have the final voice in controlling the *polis.* For all his genius, Plato died with the synthesis between philosophy and politics still largely unachieved.

Notes Chapter II

1 'The master of those who know'. *Divine Comedy, Inferno,* Canto iv, line 131.
2 For example, W. Jaeger, *The Theology of the Early Greek Philosophers* (Oxford, 1947); W. K. C. Guthrie, *In The Beginning* (Cornell, 1957); G. S. Kirk, *The Nature of Greek Myths* (Penguin Books, 1974).
3 Translation by J. Wadrington, Everyman Library edition, p. 55.
4 This is particularly noticeable in Sophocles.
5 *Iliad,* XIV, 200 and 244.
6 *Metaphysics,* A3, 983 b 27. As no genuine fragments from Thales himself have survived, a number of scholars have expressed scepticism about Aristotle's interpretation of Thales's views.
7 *Paideia,* I (Oxford, 1934), p. 152.
8 G. S. Kirk and J. E. Raven, *The Presocratic Philosophers* (Cambridge, 1957), p. 117.
9 *Heraclitus* (translation by P. Wheelwright, Princeton, 1959, p. 29).
10 Fragment 45, in Diels-Kranz, *Die Fragmente der Vorsokratiker* (5th and later editions, Berlin, 1934–54). Translation by J. B. Morrall.
11 Translation by Wheelwright, op. cit., p. 102.
12 Both were devotees of the Greek drama and of Shakespeare.
13 F. E. Peters, *Greek Philosophical Terms: An Historical Lexicon* (New York, 1967), p. 111.
14 Aristotle's explanation in the *Metaphysics* (986 b, 27–33) that Parmenides, despite himself, had to give some ground to the claims of the senses may be (as suggested by E. Hussey, *The Pre-Socratics,* London, 1972, pp. 98–9) as near to the truth as anyone is likely to get.
15 M. Untersteiner, *The Sophists* (English translation, Oxford, 1954), maintains that Gorgias's conviction of the impossibility of human mutual communication derives from a 'tragic' vision of life. While one can see some substance in Untersteiner's argument, it would seem that he understands tragedy in a somewhat narrower sense than that intended by the great Greek dramatists, even Euripides (to whom Untersteiner's remarks would most appropriately apply), and that the positive resolution of the tragic conflict by harmony between complementary forms of goodness is largely missing from Untersteiner's interpretation.
16 *Apology,* XXVIII, 38.
17 ibid., XXXII, 41 (translation by F. M. Stawell, *Socratic Discourses by Plato and Xenophon,* Everyman Library, 1910, pp. 348–9).
18 See Chapter I. It is perhaps as well to remark that, in speaking of 'Passion play', I have in mind the products of later Christendom, medieval and modern, rather than the approach taken by the Gospel narratives themselves.
19 *Apology,* XXX, 39 (Stawell, op. cit., p. 347).
20 *Crito,* XI, 50 (Stawell, op. cit., p. 359).
21 ibid., XIV, 53 (Stawell, op. cit., p. 362).

22   ibid.
23   ibid.
24   G. R. Morrow, *Plato's Cretan City*, (Princeton, 1960).

Chapter III

Aristotle in Search of
Aristoteleanism

Reliable facts on the life of Aristotle are, as in the case of other ancient philosophers, relatively scanty and dependent on indirect and late sources. The earliest known biography of Aristotle is by Hermippus of Smyrna, and dates from about a century after Aristotle's death; in other words, it is at a further remove in time than the latest of the Gospels is (on any estimate) from the death of Jesus. Furthermore, any direct knowledge of Hermippus's work is lost to us and we are dependent for anything we know about it on later extant *Lives* which made use of material contained in it. These later *Lives* divide broadly into two groups – those deriving from the biography of Hermippus and those derivative from a later biography by Ptolemy, a compiler whose date is disputed but who was probably flourishing in the fourth century AD and appears to have been a Neoplatonist. His work also has failed to achieve direct survival, but is extant in later epitomes. Ptolemy seems to have followed the general Neoplatonist tendency to attempt an ecletic harmonisation of Plato and Aristotle and his attitude to Aristotle is almost hagiographical in its partiality. In this he is doubtless influenced by the tendency of Neoplatonism to set up its philosophical pantheon of almost divine sages, perhaps as a rival to the canonised saints of Christianity. By contrast the *Lives* deriving from the tradition of Hermippus include a large degree of material critical or even abusive of Aristotle – clearly a legacy of the often bitter controversies between the philosophical schools of the third and later centuries BC.[1]

What follows is a summary of the consensus of the traditional accounts of Aristotle's life. Born in 384 at Stagira, a Greek town not far from the borders of the semi-barbarian kingdom of Macedonia, Aristotle grew up under the influence of the Hippocratic tradition of medicine which his father practised and which may well have influenced him by its emphasis on empirical investigation and respect for the evidence of concrete particularities. The *Politics* shows a number of cases of thinking on Hippocratic lines, particularly in the emphasis on taking account of geographical, topographical and climatic factors in organising the ideal *polis*.

Aristotle arrived in Athens in 367 to join Plato's Academy as a student. He stayed, so the tradition goes, for twenty years and these two decades formed the first great phase of his intellectual career. He was undoubtedly subjected to the impact of the Platonic world of thought and in fact never entirely renounced its atmosphere for the rest of his life. Dialogues in the Platonic style and other writings following with varying degrees of faithfulness in the Platonic tradition were produced by Aristotle during this period, and were well known throughout antiquity; now, however, they exist only in fragments preserved in later writings of the Graeco-Roman or even Arabic civilisations, and the authenticity and interpretation of each of them has been much discussed since their first modern publication by the nineteenth-century scholar Valentine Rose. Plato's Academy is no longer generally supposed to be the organ of propaganda of a rigidly systematic body of philosophy as was once thought; we can now appreciate that it imposed no particular 'Platonic' orthodoxy but allowed an unlimited degree of open-ended research and disputation. In this congenial atmosphere the embryonic rational genius of Aristotle could develop in ideal conditions; the freedom of inquiry which could extend even to close and critical scrutiny of Plato's own positions (which themselves, it must be remembered, were undergoing constant self-questioning, revision and even radical change) fitted in well with Aristotle's obvious wish in his extant works to explore exhaustively every facet of every question, as far, at any rate, as he saw it or allowed himself to see it.

This period of Aristotle's life came to an end with the death of Plato and the succession of Plato's nephew Speusippus to the headship of the Academy. Aristotle's departure from the Academy under its new management has sometimes been attributed to disappointment at his own failure to obtain the supreme post, but it would seem doubtful whether Aristotle, as a non-Athenian, would have stood much chance of election anyway; there would be obvious legal advantages in continuing to have an Athenian as official proprietor of the goods of the community and as its representative before the law. Another view sees political reasons (notably Aristotle's allegedly pro-Macedonian sympathies and even espionage activities) as being at the bottom of his departure from Athens;[2] but this must remain speculative. Aristotle's departure may have been based in essence on nothing more than the wanderlust shown by so many Greek thinkers. The next decade of his life is, at all events, characterised by more mobility than previously, and this is reflected intellectually in a willingness to branch out in a more personally independent direction.

The 'Academy' phase of Aristotle's thought is expressed in his so-called 'exoteric' works, intended for outside general consumption, as opposed to the 'esoteric' works, which are more academic and technical in style, and which form the basis of the *Corpus Aristotelicium* as we now have it. The 'exoteric' works were much admired in antiquity for the beauty of their style and the intellectual clarity of their exposition of philosophical topics. Unfortunately these exoteric writings were lost to sight on the downfall of Graeco-Roman civilisation. Such knowledge of them as we now have, or think we have, derives from fragments of them which were incorporated in Neoplatonic authors of the later Roman imperial period, whose syncretistic propensities have been mentioned already. The fragments which are of most interest for attempts to reconstruct the early stages of Aristotle's political thought are those which make up a treatise known as the *Protrepticus,* and which are contained in the work of a fourth-century Neoplatonist, Iamblichus, who quotes the Aristotelean fragments without acknowledgement. The best modern edition of the *Protrepticus* is by Ingemar Düring,[3] who has rearranged the fragments in what is probably the most logical manner.[4] The present author makes an act of faith in the authenticity of the fragments preserved by Iamblichus, as they do, on balance, seem to have a genuinely Aristotelean flavour.

The *Protrepticus,* as its name implies, is an exhortation. We know from a number of ancient sources that Aristotle wrote such a book for the use of Themison, a political ruler in Cyprus round about BC 350. Hardly anything is known about this figure, but the same proviso applies to Cyprian politics in general at this period. It is more to the point that the work is intended as a concise apology for the philosophical life, as understood in the rationally methodological sense sponsored by the Academy in Plato's later years. If the usually accepted dating of the *Protrepticus* is correct, the book can be regarded as the product of a man who had been connected with the Academy for nearly two decades. It is no production of a tyro and it may even have been an officially encouraged attempt to gain publicity for the Academy's case in a new *milieu.* The Cyprian destination of the work would, on this assumption, be significant, for the Academy's great Athenian educational rival, Isocrates, who favoured a more traditional rhetorical system of training, had long before attempted to publicise his method in Cyprus by writing several protreptical discourses to Nicocles, a young Cyprian king, in the 370s. Aristotle would on this analysis be trying, on the Academy's behalf, to offset the long-standing prestige and influence of the Isocratean school on the island.

The twentieth-century German scholar Werner Jaeger, in his influential interpretation of Aristotle's intellectual history,[5] contended that the *Protrepticus* reveals Aristotle as a wholehearted Platonist, arguing for philosophy as supplying a practical yardstick for providing infallible rules for correct political behaviour, somewhat as Plato had tried to do in the *Republic*. Other scholars, notably Düring, have maintained that some of the intellectual motifs of the *Protrepticus* are already non-Platonic, particularly the concept of Nature, which is said to herald one of the basic tenets of mature Aristoteleanism. A glance through what we have of the *Protrepticus* according to Düring's arrangement may serve to provide orientation in this controversy.

Aristotle begins by insisting on the indispensability of philosophy for everyday life. No one can use the external goods of life without proper training in the ultimate purpose for which they are given to mankind; happiness is no mere process of acquiring material possessions for their own sake. This certainly strikes a very similar note to the treatment of happiness in Book I of the *Nicomachean Ethics*. A similar Aristotelean flavour occurs in the effort to distinguish between two different connotations of the verb 'to philosophise': 'the word "philosophise" means both "to inquire whether we ought to philosophise or not" and "to devote oneself to philosophical speculation" '.[6] At the same time an undoubted Platonic legacy is also clear in this pregnant system. Plato too in a number of dialogues (for example in those examined in our previous chapter) had distinguished between the methodology and *raison d'être* of philosophy on the one hand and its subject matter on the other.

A more distinctively Aristotelean note seems to be struck in the appeal to nature as providing the guidelines on which philosophy prescribes 'what ought to be done or not to be done'.[7] We have already seen the contrast sharpened by some fifth-century thinkers between 'nature' and 'law', and Aristotle, like Plato, is obviously trying here to argue for the essential harmony of the two concepts. Philosophy is to act as Nature's instrument in prescribing a moral code.

The subsequent discussion on the teleological character of Nature is even more redolent of mature Aristotelean thinking. 'We should assume that everything that comes into being rightly comes into being for an end';[8] Aristotle admits, as he does in his *Physics*, that the element of chance in the natural world cannot be ignored or pronounced, *à la* Parmenides, to be non-existent; what he refuses to admit is that chance and its products are good in the strict sense of the term, i.e. as serving a logical purpose. The natural purpose of Man, he goes on to argue, is to pursue wisdom, because this pursuit entails the exercise of Man's noblest functions, his mental powers, which are the last components in a human being to develop and hence are the highest expressions of human life. Aristotle works on the belief that growth (which is of course a standard meaning of *physis*, the Greek 'nature') is a process of development within time, which carries with it the corollary that the chronologically later is the naturally superior, at any rate until all the essential features of a given organism have received full expression. A modern might perhaps scoff at this conception as *naif* or mechanical, but to Aristotle it was essential for his vindication, primarily against Parmenides, of change, time and movement as realities to be reckoned with once more by philosophy, and this restoration of reality to time and the child of time, history (anticipated to a sizeable extent by Plato) was obviously of tremendous significance to any systematic investigation of politics. Among other effects it was to heal the breach between the poetic and philosophical traditions which had so unhappily, as we have seen, parted company in the fifth century.

Aristotle's next objective in the *Protrepticus* is to show that the pursuit of wisdom, as the exercise most appropriate to the rational faculty of Man, is the highest and best activity of a human being. Even moral virtue (*arete*) is to be pursued for the sake of wisdom, 'for wisdom is the supreme end'.[9] Thus thoughts which are pursued for the sake of reason are those (as Aristotle says in strange anticipation of Hegel) which are most free; Aristotle's conception of freedom applies only to those intellectual or practical elements which are self-contained and self-subsistent in the teleological scale of being or knowledge; thus Aristotle implicitly rejects any indeterminacy, of the type often so dear to modern liberal thought, in the notion of freedom and anchors the concept firmly to that of purpose. So pure thinking (to define which Aristotle follows Plato by using the term *dianoia*),[10] 'is more honourable and better than thinking directed towards receiving some advantage'.[11] This is, according to Aristotle, the distinctive property of Man: 'Animals have some small sparks of reason and prudence [*logos* and *phronesis*] but are entirely deprived of theoretical wisdom [*sophia*].'[12] Here a new and important theme enters the discussion – the drawing of a distinction between *phronesis* and *sophia*. Later, in the *Corpus Aristotelicum* itself, Aristotle develops this into his famous division between the practical and theoretical sciences, which marks a considerable break with Platonism's normal attitude. The latter had assumed an indivisibility between the different branches of knowledge, just as it assumed a basic identity between the different ethical types of goodness, instead of the pluralism which

46

was on the whole favoured by mature Aristoteleanism. The interest of this passage of the *Protrepticus* is in the picture which it suggests of Aristotle groping his way towards what he will eventually feel to be a more comprehensive philosophical map of reality than that provided by Plato, even though he works largely towards the same objectives as his one-time master and is never far away from the legacy of Platonism.

One of the lasting ambiguities of the legacy crops up in another section of the *Protrepticus*.[13] Aristotle's rather oscillating method of argument here, together with his somewhat imprecise use of key terms such as *phronesis* and *sophia*, suggest that he is still of two minds in his attitude towards Platonism, now receiving its most monumental expression in the *Laws*. The influence of the latest and in many ways most influential phase of Plato's development (his attempt in the *Laws* to combine cosmology and politics, law and philosophy in an over-arching synthesis) is clearly visible in the younger philosopher's more tentative and sketchy argument in the *Protrepticus*, where Aristotle contends, somewhat awkwardly when judged by strictly logical standards, that wisdom (*phronesis* again) is the most useful as well as the greatest of all goods,[14] that the most excellent (*spoudaios*) ought to rule because he 'is by his nature strongest'[15] and, somewhat dis-crepantly, that 'the law alone is ruler and has authority',[16] because it is the embodiment of *phronesis*. This vacillation between opting for the wise man (who possesses *phronesis*) and the law would be natural to one still under the spell of Plato's former ideal of government by all-wise experts and yet one who, like Plato himself, was coming to see the growingly grave objections to that ideal. On the whole, the earlier Platonic ideal is still, by a strange paradox, flourishing more strongly in the attitude of the early Aristotle than of the later Plato. Fragment B40[17] shows Aristotle even talking in terms of the psycho-logy of the *Republic*, which Plato himself had by now largely outgrown and abandoned. Again in B42[18] Aristotle seems to take up an anti-utilitarian attitude which is hard to reconcile not only with his own professed objective in the *Protrepticus* of showing the practical political use of philosophy, but also from the more realistic outlook of Plato in his later dialogues. The austerity of Aristotle's standpoint here may be gauged by a passage such as: 'To seek from all know-ledge a result other than itself and to demand that knowledge must be useful is the act of one completely ignorant of the distance that from the start separates things good from things necessary; they stand at opposite extremes.'[19] In a chain argument, reminiscent of his famous proof of the existence of the Unmoved Mover, God, in the *Metaphysics*,[20] he declares:

47

. . . those [goods] that are loved for themselves, even if nothing else follows from them, must be called goods in the strict sense; for this is not desirable for the sake of that, and that for the sake of something else, and so *ad infinitum*; there is a stop somewhere. It is really ridiculous, then, to demand from everything some benefit besides the thing itself, and to ask 'What then is the gain to us?' and 'What is the use?'[21]

Aristotle seems however to want to have his cake and eat it, for a little later we find him[22] maintaining that 'theoretical insight' (*theoretikos phronesis*) is of the greatest use for practical life. The combination of the two Greek words quoted, a combination which would be anathema to the Aristotle of the *Corpus*, is an indication of the uneven progress of Aristotle towards defining a consistent independent approach towards the relationship of contemplative wisdom and social ethics. By the same token the separation of theory from *phronesis* in later Aristotelean thought would be indicative of the solution for which Aristotle was, at first unconsciously, looking.

Even at his most confused here, however, Aristotle still keeps a firm hold of his main contention that Nature must be the criterion of legitimate as well as effective action in the crafts as well as in politics. His argument is that only the philosopher copies Nature at first hand; other practitioners of arts and crafts do so at various indirect stages, and they therefore rely on experience. It is not clear why experience should not be of a direct kind, but Aristotle is obviously anxious to confine exact rational knowledge to the theoretical plane and to exclude any sort of empirically determined judgements from the highest rung of the hierarchical ladder of reasoning. Empirical limitation of goodness is, for him, not on the same level as direct rational contact with it. A comparison of theoretical knowledge with the faculty of eyesight is taken to prove that all practice can be framed in accordance with theory of the most uncompromisingly contemplative kind.

This approach leads Aristotle into another apparent paradox. Philosophy achieves its perfection not, as we might expect, through undiluted contemplative thought, but through being practically useful as a means towards active virtue. This is something of a surprise and the whole argument here[23] is somewhat discordant with what has gone before. But it serves to illustrate the insistence of Aristotle, even at this comparatively early stage in his intellectual career, on preserving an essential link between philosophy and practical life, particularly politics. The immediately following assertion that 'all men feel at home in philosophy and wish to spend their lives in the pursuit of it',[24] though exaggeratedly optimistic, as one would think, shows Aristotle moving almost towards a democratic theory of the acquisition of knowledge, with every man his own philosopher. He is obviously far from the elitism of Plato as well as from his own later brand, noticeable in the *Ethics* (both versions) and the *Politics*. The concept of a person of practical insight who need not necessarily be a contemplative philosopher had not yet been fully worked out by Aristotle. The *phronimos* ('man possessing *phronesis*') who was finally to fit the bill in the *Ethics* had not yet attained his full potentialities in Aristotle's thought. At the moment, in the *Protrepticus*, Aristotle struggles to square the circle of belief in teleologically unconditioned philosophical speculation (i.e. philosophy with no end beyond its own activity) with the equally strongly held belief that the supreme good must also be the supremely useful. Logically speaking, the attempt is doomed to failure and one sees that eventually Aristotle was bound to fall back on his later classically formulated position in the *Corpus* whereby different branches of knowledge, theoretical and practical, were carefully distinguished, and the sphere of utility strictly confined to the practical sciences.

In B67–8[25] Aristotle is back to pursuing the thesis that philosophy is the highest type of knowledge precisely because 'it is impossible to imagine that its end is to produce something'.[26] It is therefore of supreme value in its own right. The analogy between theoretical knowledge and the light of physical vision, so reminiscent of Plato, leads to the argument that philosophical knowledge is a kind of perception and, like all perfection, is valued in its own right (because life would be impossible without perception, whether of the senses or the intellect); philosophical knowledge is a higher form of perception even than physical sight.

A new approach to the problem of why, if philosophy is possible for all, so few actually embark on it, is implicitly contained in the distinction which Aristotle makes between potentiality and actuality. This again was to become a characteristic theme of his mature philosophy, and was to enable him to combine a nominal universalist humanism with a practical elitism, a combination which was to form a crucial element in his political theory. In this case, with echoes this time of Heraclitus, Aristotle contrasts active philosophical thought with dormant philosophical capacity (possessed by all) by using an analogy, just as Heraclitus had done, the obvious physical contrast between a human being awake and one asleep. Plato's recognition of the positive importance of dreams for human psychology (shown in a number of dialogues, for example the *Republic* and the *Timaeus*) is by-passed, perhaps deliberately; its admission would have somewhat impaired the validity of the analogy used by Aristotle. Aristotle contents himself with arguing that sleep is a state of complete illusion for the soul: 'the images of sleep are false, while those of waking life are true. For sleep and waking differ in nothing else but the fact that the soul when awake often knows the truth, but in sleep is always deceived; for the whole nature of dreams is an image and unreal.'[27] The more realistic attitude of Plato to dreams in *Republic* IX is a great contrast to Aristotle's rather rigorist attitude here.

The *Protrepticus* viewed as a whole certainly reveals fundamental ambiguities both in argument and underlying purpose. These ambiguities may be traced to an indecision on the real function of the human soul, an indecision which Aristotle copes with more successfully in the *Corpus* but never fully makes consistent. Without the tripartite conception which Plato used in the *Republic* and elsewhere, and without his own later careful distinctions between the various faculties of the unitary soul in *De Anima,* Aristotle is driven to a one-sided emphasis on the rational and indeed immortal character of the disembodied soul and a consequent pessimism with regard to all human temporal activity. The gruesome image of the soul chained to the body as the Etruscans tortured captives by yoking the dead in a face-to-face confrontation with the living seems to Aristotle at this phase to sum up the body-soul relationship, and one is not surprised to find hints[28] of acceptance of Empedocles's theories and those of the Mystery Religions (Orphism, etc.) that existence itself is a penalty for previous sins of the soul, for which it must atone by being connected with the flesh. At the end of the treatise one feels more than ever uncertain about Aristotle's attitude towards human earthly life. A desire to be off at all costs from the irksome round of human temporal norm, and the conviction that philosophy is the only way of attaining this Nirvana-like condition would seem to ensure that Aristotle would be a non-starter in any attempt to give a positive intellectual evaluation to the problems and needs of political life. The road from the *Protrepeticus* would seem logically to lead to regions where the very idea of a 'political philosophy' would appear to be a contradiction in terms.

Yet Aristotle did not eventually take such a road. Between the day when he left Athens and broke official connection with the Academy (347 BC)[29] and the time when he returned in the wake of the Macedonian conquest ten years later to found the Lyceum, Aristotle's thought underwent profound changes. The causes for the change may have been several in number.

First of all may be placed his residence in north-western Asia Minor and the adjacent islands. His main, though not exclusive, place of residence during this decade of absence from Athens was the court of Hermias of Atarneus, a tyrant of a petty but strategically crucial city state in the controversial border region between the Persian Empire and the rising new Macedonian kingdom. Aristotle married the tyrant's daughter and it has been suggested that he formed a part of a pro-Macedonian circle which had Hermias as its centre and which had as its objective the provision of a territorial bridgehead in Asia which would facilitate the invasion of the Persian dominions contemplated by Philip and carried out with overwhelming success by Alexander. Certainly here Aristotle was living at the heart of practical political plan and counter-plan and the execution of Hermias by the Persians must have hit him hard. A poem by Aristotle in memory of Hermias praises the latter's bravery and patriotism.

Aristotle's stay in the islands of north-west Asia Minor, particularly Lesbos, produced another significant orientation. Following the investigation of his biological writings by D'Arcy Thompson earlier in this century,[30] which showed that most of Aristotle's practical observations of marine and other forms of animal life must have been made in this area, it would seem that this period of his life must have seen the elaboration of his technique of empirical biological observation which introduced into his thought a practical element of induction differentiating him from much of the previous Greek philosophical tradition and perhaps particularly from Plato. Dr Marjorie Grene, in her *Portrait of Aristotle*,[31] argues very convincingly that this biological orientation of Aristotle determined his whole outlook towards physical science in every field he studied and, more important still, moulded decisively and permanently his whole philosophical stance because, to quote Dr Grene, '. . . *living*[32] nature is made the focal point of philosophical reflection . . .'.[33] In other words, the fact that Aristotle served his apprenticeship in scientific investigation largely as a biologist provided him with what would have appeared to him to be factual foundation for the inspired guess at the essentially purposive and orderly character of Nature which we have already found adumbrated in the *Protrepticus*. The wonderful adaptation of animal and marine organisms to their environment, the classic and unique character of the genera and species of the sub-human world (which Aristotle was prepared, as no other thinker before him anywhere had been, to study attentively and even affectionately),[34] made it impossible for him to believe that the universe as a whole was a product of random combination of blindly motiveless forces. Nor could it be reduced to the changeless and undifferentiated uniformity of Parmenides. Aristotle did in fact deliver the final *coup de grâce* to any chance of a Parmenidean takeover of Greek and therefore European philosophy. The answer, the real clinching argument to otherthrow Parmenides, was found by Aristotle in his perception, inspired by biology, of real continuity in real change which he expressed in his theory of the universe as teleological, with every one of its parts moving forward to actualise its specific potentiality, to realise its own unique character, to obtain its own distinctive perfection which would follow from the exercise of its true function. The fourfold theory of causation (material, formal, efficient and final) furnished a ladder of connecting collaboration between lowlier and higher elements in the universal structure. In Matter, the shapeless but necessary basis of all the colourful diversity of life, Aristotle saw the prophecy of Form, the shaping of meaningful functioning organisms, while the work of the author of the process, the efficient cause, the agent which gave impetus to this natural development was linked in its turn to the final purposive goal to which everything in this chain of life was moving.

Aristotle's teleology has been a feature of his philosophy which has been subjected to much criticism, particularly on the ground that it imputes an unverifiable moral purpose to the workings of the universe. Recently there has been a trend to 'rescue' Aristotle from the ultimate implications of his teleology by arguing that it is a conception which must be interpreted in a strictly relative manner, conditioned by the particular mode of being which is under consideration. No absolute scheme of interpreting the *whole* of reality on teleological lines is intended by Aristotle, so the argument runs.[35] When Aristotle does appear to be talking in 'theological' terms about a general unified teleological purpose linking the entire universe, this school of thought interprets such evidence as symbolistic window-dressing.[36] The more traditional 'face value' interpretation of Aristotle's teleological theories in the light of Metaphysics would seem to the present writer to remain as still the more plausible alternative.

Whatever the interpretation of this problem, the main consequence of Aristotle's teleology remains clear. It enabled him to face the possibility of change, whether in cosimc or human affairs, by viewing it as a continuous unfolding of essential constants arising from the nature of the organism concerned. Aristotle does not of course see this process in terms of modern evolution, with its overwhelming emphasis on change as adaptation for the sake of survival. In Aristotle's biological and physical universe the general pattern of divisions and types of being, vegetable, animal, human and celestial, are fixed once and for all, and such changes as may occur are modifications within this overall framework, not movements outside it altogether, due to innovating factors making for species transformation. This limited framework *is* limited precisely because limitation is for Aristotle an indispensable condition for defining and classifying the unique status of each type of being within its own terms of development. He expresses this fundamental tenet of his thought very clearly in the opening sections of the *Politics,* in the context of his definition of the *polis*: ' . . . the "nature" of things consists in their end or consummation; for what each thing is when its growth is completed we call the nature of that thing, whether it be a man or a horse or a family'.[37] It follows that as soon as any grade of being in the Aristotelean universe has reached its full capacity of development in realising its own nature, conservation rather than change is its primary need. Further attempts at change beyond this optimum point would not only be useless and superfluous for the organism concerned; they would in addition bring about a positive deterioration because they would be an unnatural attempt to go outside the nature governing the correct functional status of the organism. For this reason Aristotle criticises a number of aspects of the *polis* structure of his own time; the *polis* has for him reached its natural term of development and a policy of enlightened conservatism is therefore regarded by him throughout the *Politics* as the primary need for the stabilisation of the Greek cities of his own time. This conservatism in turn entails a respect for, and careful study of, the political opinions and traditions of the past. As in theoretical philosophy, so in the practical sciences like ethics and politics, the original thinker must also first be a scholar, a skilled interpreter of what is of lasting value in previous ideas and explanations in the field concerned. The Aristotelean man of learning, even more than his Platonist counterpart, cannot ultimately work alone; he needs to live and think within a community of like-minded persons, dedicated to establishing and sifting the evidence of the past in order to act to the most rational (and therefore most naturally correct) effect in the present and the future.

This co-operative character of Aristoteleanism is responsible for some of the difficulty surrounding the interpretation of the works composing what we now know as the *Corpus Aristotelicum.* These were known in antiquity as the 'esoteric' works of the philosopher (in contrast to the 'exoteric' works, such as the *Protrepticus,* intended for a more general public); they are clearly not meant to be finished and polished treatises, conveying the last word on the subjects they discuss; they are rather notes, more or less rough, intended for fellow philosophers and students, tabulating, arranging and when possible giving provisional answers to questions in every field of knowledge surveyed by Aristotle's 'Peripatetic' school.

53

It would seem likely that most of the *Corpus,* at any rate in the arrangement in which we have it, dates from the years of Aristotle's second and final stay in Athens from the Macedonian conquest in 338 to the death of Alexander the Great in 323 and the subsequent anti-Macedonian rising which forced Aristotle to flee from the city, to prevent (as one source reports him as remarking) the Athenians from committing a second crime against philosophy (the first being the execution of Socrates). The setting up of the Lyceum at the beginning of this last and most significant period of Aristotle's career marked an attempt by the philosopher to form a permanent basis and institution for the propagation of his methods and ideas, but the exact nature of the institution and its workings is still relatively obscure, and much that earlier modern scholarship took for granted has, as in the case of Plato's Academy, more recently been challenged. The recent careful study of J. P. Lynch, *Aristotle's School: A study of a Greek educational institution*[38] collects and evaluates all the available evidence and makes what seems to be the most plausible overall attempt so far to interpret it convincingly. It is clear that neither the Academy nor the Lyceum were corporate institutions resembling the medieval or modern universities; in the case of the Lyceum, the fact that Aristotle, as a resident alien, did not hold, and legally never could hold, Athenian citizenship prevented his school from purchasing landed property which would have stabilised its position. This was all the more unfortunate because Aristotelean methodology, with its respect for the fund of knowledge available from the past in any intellectual field, needed more than any other of the philosophical schools a library as an indispensable working tool. Unlike Plato, who doubted the possibility of expressing ultimate philosophical truth in writing, Aristotle had from his Academy days realised the importance of continuous contact with past reflective thought which only the study of its written heritage could provide; there is a pleasant story in one of the ancient *Lives* which tells of Plato calling Aristotle 'the Reader' in gentle irony. As Lynch puts it: 'The lack of privately owned school property undoubtedly presented a difficult problem for the Peripatetics. Just to house Aristotle's own writings and notes, considerable space would have been required.'[39] The problem was solved only after Aristotle's death, when his successor as head of the Lyceum, Theophrastus of Lesbos, succeeded in obtaining permission from a former pupil, Demetrius of Phalerum, who became for a while dictator of Athens under the aegis of Macedonia, to own the patch of public ground at the Lyceum which Aristotle had unofficially occupied as his philosophical headquarters.[40] Theophrastus's will followed the strange course of leaving the whole of the library in private ownership to a member of the school, Neleus, who, probably in pique at not being elected to succeed Theophrastus, took the library away to his native city of Skepsis, in north-west Asia Minor. The decline and probable extinction (according to Lynch) of the Athenian Lyceum during the third century BC was probably in large measure due to the loss of the library, as well as political disorders in Hellenistic Athens. The tradition of Aristotelean philosophy was preserved outside Athens at centres like Alexandria, while the *Corpus* (as it was eventually to become) passed through a number of dramatic vicissitudes after its inheritance by Neleus and eventually appeared at Rome in the first century BC to form the basis of our present text of Aristotle.

The close co-operation as a body of members of the Aristotelean school has raised the question in modern years as to how much of what we know as the works of Aristotle are his own personal product. It would certainly be rash to assert that all the *Corpus* as we have it is undisputably by Aristotle himself; in the twentieth century, more than previously, it has become clear that the treatises embody various layers of chronological composition manifesting themselves in the final redaction in differences of emphasis and even definite inconsistency of meaning. This 'genetic' approach to the study of Aristotle's writings which has held the field since the appearance of W. Jaeger's famous *Aristotle* in 1923 would now be generally accepted though it need not preclude a systematic 'structural' approach to the writings which would emphasise the continuity and unity of the thought which they express. An extremely radical wing of the 'genetic' approach has attempted more recently to argue that the *Corpus* is not by Aristotle himself but by Aristotelians of the next (Theophrastean) generation or even later.[41] Acceptance of this suggestion would lead to the strange position that the main writings left to be ascribed to the founder of the Peripatetic school would be the 'exoteric' treatises, which would mean that Aristotle's place in the history of philosophy would be limited to that of a maverick and not too well-known member of the Platonist school. This conclusion seems at variance with the estimate of Aristotle's philosophical originality given by ancient sources, and on the whole is not very probable. For what it is worth, and with all due allowance for subjectivity, it remains the case that the overwhelming majority of interpreters of Aristotle have been impressed with the appearance of organisation by a single mind which is conveyed by the *Corpus*, even in the baffling and sometimes barely readable form in which it has come down to us. As far as the *Politics* is concerned, the theory of post-Aristotelean composition is even less convincing than in the case of other parts of the *Corpus*, because precise references to historical political happenings are made.

As the latest of these is to an event in 336 BC, it seems unlikely that the work can date from a period well after the death of Aristotle.

The main virtue of the 'genetic' school, even in its wilder flights of interpretation, has been to direct attention to the process of development behind the Aristotelean works, as well as to the structural unity of system emphasised by older commentators. We shall try to bear both approaches in mind as we turn to examine the specific development of Aristotle's discourses on the political world and of the human personalities which compose and determine it.

Notes Chapter III

1 The most thorough modern attempt to sift whatever assured facts can be extracted from these baffling sources is that of I. Düring, *Aristotle in the Ancient Biographical Tradition* (Göteborg, 1957) (in English). An interesting effort to interpret the evidence in novel and often speculative senses is made by A.-H. Chroust, *Aristotle*, Vol. I (London, 1973).
2 So Chroust, op. cit., *passim*.
3 *Aristotle's Protrepticus: An attempt at reconstruction* (Göteborg, 1961).
4 It should be pointed out that a minority of reputable scholarly opinion still holds that there is no certain proof that the Iamblichus fragments are genuinely Aristotelean; see e.g. G. Rabinowitz, *Aristotle's Protrepticus and the Sources of its Reconstruction* (Berkeley and Los Angeles, 1957), and C. J. Rowe, *The Eudemian and Nicomachean Ethics: A study in the development of Aristotle's thought* (Cambridge, 1971).
5 *Aristotle: Fundamentals of the history of his development* (English translation) (2nd edn, Oxford, 1948).
6 Fragment B6, p. 49, in Düring's edition of the *Protrepticus*, op. cit., as above. All translations of the Greek text are from Düring's version as in this edition.
7 Düring, op. cit., p. 51.
8 ibid., p. 53.
9 ibid., p. 57. Düring here uses 'wisdom' as a translation of *phronesis*, which Aristotle later uses with the meaning of 'practical insight or understanding' as distinct from *sophia*, which indicates wisdom with a more contemplative and theoretical meaning.
10 See e.g. Plato's allegory of the Line in *Republic*, VI.
11 Düring, op. cit., p. 59.
12 ibid.
13 ibid., pp. 63–7.
14 ibid., p. 63.
15 ibid. Is Aristotle here trying to steal the thunder by stealing the vocabulary of the 'immoralist' school of Sophist thought? The reference to natural strength might lead one to suspect so.
16 ibid.
17 ibid., p. 63.

18 ibid., p. 65.
19 B42, ibid., p. 65.
20 Book Lambda.
21 *Protepticus*, B42, Düring, op. cit., p. 65.
22 B46, ibid., p. 67.
23 B52–3, ibid., p. 71.
24 B56, ibid., p. 73.
25 ibid., p. 77.
26 B69, ibid.
27 B202, ibid., p. 89.
28 B206, ibid., p. 91.
29 Chroust, op. cit., Vol. I, pp. 117–24, contends that the cause for
    Aristotle's departure was political and the consequence of his known
    pro-Macedonian sympathies. But this seems far from certain.
30 D'Arcy Thompson, notes to Oxford translation of *Historia Animalium*
    (1910); *Greek Birds* (2nd edn, 1936); *Greek Fishes* (1947).
31 London, 1963.
32 Dr Grene's italics.
33 *Portrait of Aristotle*, pp. 227–8.
34 See the famous apologia for biological studies in *De Partibus
    Animalium*, I, v, 664 b 22–645 a 36.
35 In this sense, W. Wieland, *Die aristotelische Physik* (2nd edn, Göttingen,
    1970), ch. 16; translated into English as 'The Problem of Teleology' in
    J. Barnes, M. Schofield and R. Sorabji, (eds), (London, 1975), pp.
    141–60.
36 For example, Wieland, op. cit., p. 158: 'I am inclined to view all
    passages in the treatises which hint at a theological basis for natural
    teleology, or in which nature appears as a being which plans and acts,
    as concessions to popular notions, which do not touch the kernel of
    Aristotle's thought.'
37 *Politics*, I, ii, 1252 b (translation by E. Barker, *The Politics of Aristotle*,
    Oxford, 1948, p. 5).
38 Berkeley and Los Angeles, 1972.
39 Lynch, op. cit., p. 97.
40 Lynch, op. cit., p. 46 points out: 'Well before Aristotle became
    associated with the place, the Lyceum was being used for a large number
    of concurrent functions, not the least of which was its role as an
    educational center where traditional and innovative practices found a
    proving ground.'
41 The principal expositions of this view are in J. Zürcher, *Aristoteles'
    Werk und Geist* (Paderborn, 1952); A.-H. Chroust, *Aristotle: New
    light on his life and on some of his lost works*, 2 vols (London, 1973);
    F. Grayeff, *Aristotle and his School* (London, 1974).

Chapter IV

Political Science, Peripatetic Style

A long-standing misapprehension about Aristotle's treatment of politics is that it is a field of inquiry separate from, even if closely connected with, his ethical system. In actual fact there is no textual evidence whatever to warrant the belief that Aristotle knew any separate science of ethics. For him individual ethical behaviour is a subdivision of what he terms 'political science', an overall intellectual exploration of the inseparable fields of both individual and communal life which together make up the unit of the *polis*.[1]

In our discussion of Aristotle's political outlook, we shall concentrate on the textual evidence provided by the *Nicomachean Ethics* and the *Politics* itself. Although aware of definite differences in content and emphasis between the *Nicomachean* and *Eudemian Ethics* we shall in this chapter limit our interpretation to the former, which treats Aristotle's ethical concepts in greater detail and which also has more connection with the discussion in the *Politics*.[2]

Discussion in the *Ethics*[3] presupposes the distinction between the theoretical sciences (i.e. forms of purely contemplative knowledge) and the practical sciences (forms of knowledge issuing in useful action). To the former belong studies such as metaphysics, physics, and so on, to the latter studies like ethics, politics and rhetoric. Each group is arranged on hierarchical lines, with a master science summing up and supplying the purpose for subordinate sciences. At the beginning of the *Ethics* political science is stated to be the chief of the practical sciences. This is because it seeks the means for the good of the whole community, which must take precedence over that of individuals composing it: 'This is not to deny that the good of the individual is worth while. But what is good for a nation or a city has a higher, a diviner quality.'[4] At first sight there would seem to be here a certain downgrading of contemplative philosophy which, as an undeniably individual pursuit, would seem as a result to be ranked below the science of communal good which is politics. But we must remember that politics is one, even if the chief, of the practical sciences, which are ranked below the theoretical sciences.

A consequence of this *practical* status of politics is that it can never be an exact science as can mathematics or metaphysics: 'we must be content if we attain as high a degree of certainty as the matter of it admits'.[5] This means that the conclusions of politics are to be sought primarily in experience rather than deductive knowledge. A by-product of this fact, according to Aristotle, is that politics 'is not a proper study for the young. The young man is not versed in the practical business of life from which politics draws its premises and data. He is besides swayed by his feelings with the result that he will make no headway and derive no benefit from a study the end of which is not knowing but doing.'[6] Aristotle seems here to take the opposite position to Plato in the *Republic*, for whom practical experience in the service of the state was a necessary preliminary before philosophy could be embarked upon. Aristotle, however, holds here that some grasp of first principles must be necessary before study of ethics and politics can profitably be undertaken.

For Aristotle the first principle of ethics is that it is directed towards achieving happiness for the individual, a happiness achieved in the correct functioning of his human powers. This is not an entirely individualist ideal, for Aristotle makes clear that by being self-sufficient is meant 'not what is sufficient for oneself living the life of a solitary but includes parents, wife and children, friends and fellow-citizens in general. For man is a social animal.'[7] So there is a necessary interconnection of individual and communal life, which for Aristotle means a close relationship between ethics and politics. In fact for Aristotle the connection is so close that he can define the task of political government in what appear to be exclusively ethical terms: 'What the statesman is most anxious to produce is a certain moral character in his fellow-citizens, namely a disposition to virtue and the performance of virtuous actions.'[8] 'The genuine statement is – a man who has taken peculiar pains to master this problem [i.e. what happiness is], desiring as he does to make his fellow-citizens good men obedient to the laws.'[9] So 'the study of moral goodness is a part of political science'.[10]

This political inculcation of virtue operates chiefly through the imparting by the government to its subjects of correct habits. 'We find legislators seeking to make good men of their fellows by making good behaviour habitual with them. That is the aim of every lawgiver, and when he is unable to carry it out effectively, he is a failure; nay, success or failure in this is what makes the difference between a good constitution and a bad.'[11]

The interconnection between ethics and politics is shown by the pre-eminence in both of the faculty of *phronesis* or practical prudence (to be distinguished from *sophia,* or wisdom derived from theoretical contemplative of absolute truth). The *Ethics* is concerned with stating points which may serve as useful guides in acquiring and preserving such prudence, e.g. the use of a central position between opposites as a yardstick – the famous 'Golden Mean', e.g. bravery as the mean between cowardice (a lack of the virtue of courage) and rashness (an excess of it). This idea of the mean is also expressed in the *Politics* – the 'polity' as the mean between two extremes of oligarchy and democracy. Aristotle insists, however, that the mean is no magic formula – it partakes of all the uncertainties of the world of practical knowledge, together with the particular hazards which the possession of free choice attaches to all human behaviour by an ultimate residuum of unpredictability. *Phronesis,* the supreme virtue in politics as well as ethics, rests on the application of a central standard of sanity in a million varied and unpredictable circumstances. No cast-iron rules can be given; but the way to salvation lies through the training of the practical intellect through acquired experience and habit to choose the right course of action in each particular case which may come up.

The rejection of any doctrinaire standpoint in ethics and politics is proof of the intellectual journey travelled by Aristotle since the *Protrepticus,* when he would, if he could, have awarded all political power to the contemplative philosopher. We can see that Nature, which in the *Protrepticus* had tended to be a pattern of clear-cut rules apprehended by philosophical contemplation, is now (for the Aristotle of the *Ethics* and *Politics*) nearer the modern sense of the word – a shorthand term for the incalculable and unpredictable variety of life. In this jungle of unpredictables and uncertainties, Man possesses a unique faculty – that of rational and deliberate choice. The emphasis on this attribute, which is for Aristotle the ground of differentiation between Man and the rest of biological life, makes him in this aspect a philosopher of both ethical and political freedom. Mature choice occupies for him in ethics and politics the same key position as Plato had assigned to possession of correct knowledge. Though Aristotle did not always see all the practical consequences of his position, his view was obviously closer to the current practice of the Greek *polis* than was Plato's. It was not however very reconcilable with the absolute monarchical government of Hellenistic and imperial Roman times, and this may account partly for the greater vogue enjoyed by Platonic ideas during those periods. Aristotle had to wait for the later Middle Ages, with their relative widening of participation in the governing process, to become a popular authority.

Choice is defined by Aristotle as 'the deliberate desire of something within our power'.[12] This suffices to place the exercise of choice firmly within the field of the practical sciences. Aristotle insists that 'it is about things which we can influence by our action that we deliberate. Nobody deliberates about eternal things, such as the stellar system or the incommensurability of the diagonal with the side of a square.'[13] One might study these things in contemplation but clearly they cannot be affected by deliberation or choice on our part. 'Deliberation then is concerned with things which, while in general following certain definite lines, have no predictable issues, or the result of which cannot be clearly stated.'[14] Aristotle also argues that we do not deliberate about ends but always about means. A doctor does not deliberate whether or not he will cure his patients, nor an orator whether or not he is to win over his audience, nor a statesman whether or not he is to produce law and order, nor does anyone else deliberate about the end at which he is aiming.[15] He takes it for granted. The end is of course for Aristotle a built-in urge towards development inherent in every process and no more choosable than one's own coming into existence. This is why in his political thought Aristotle spends very little time in justifying the existence of the political community; it is there for him from the start as an inescapable and essential part of human development. The discussion of the origins of the *polis* in *Politics*, Book I, is an answer to the 'How?' rather than the 'Why?' of the beginnings of political life.

This relativism, dictated both by the flexibility of the subject matter (the practical sciences) and by the human instruments operating upon them (prudence issuing in choice), is a fundamental attribute of Aristotle's approach to politics. He is keenly aware that the relativism may even lead very often to a clash between the *phronesis* of an individual and that of a *polis*: to be a good man and to be a good citizen may not necessarily be identical. (In the *Politics* Aristotle will contend that only in fact in the ideal *polis* is such an assimilation certain.) This means that political science is to abandon exorbitant claims to pre-eminence among subjects of knowledge: 'I find it stranger that any should regard political science or *practical* wisdom as the noblest of studies, for that is to assume that Man is what is best in the universe'.[16] Aristotle's cosmology placed a number of super-intelligent beings, the intelligences governing the stars and planets above Man in the scale of being, as well as God, the Unmoved Mover. This is the sphere of contemplative Wisdom.

Prudence is just as necessary as wisdom for the conduct of life and within the sphere of prudence experience is as important as theory.

A man is aware that light meats are easily digested and beneficial to health but does not know what meats are light. Such a man is not likely to make you as well as one who only knows that chicken is good for you. It is in fact experience rather than theory that normally gets results. Practical wisdom being concerned with action, we need both kinds of knowledge; nay, we need the knowledge of particular facts more than general principles. But here too there must be a faculty – political science – in which the ultimate authority is vested.[17]

In the *Ethics* Aristotle distinguishes between two branches of political science – (a) 'legislative', the higher, and (b) 'political', more properly speaking dealing with administrative details. The latter is the sphere of practical politicians who ' bear the same relation to the lawgiver as workman to the master-craftsman'.[18] Here there is an interesting return to the *Protrepticus* analogy between guiding principles in arts and crafts and the subordinate working out of them in detail. Aristotle seems to be arguing for a distinction between the man of *phronesis*, the ethical philosopher, and the practical politician, who puts into effect the recommendations of the possessor of *phronesis*. Once again we seem to be within shouting distance of Platonic government by experts, except that with Aristotle the character of the expert is different. For him the ruling type of mind must be, not the philosopher as such, but the man of *phronesis*, the possessor of prudence tested by experience, the philosopher of the practical sciences. Aristotle indicates the difference by a clear denial that his system gives prudence precedence over wisdom, the faculty applying to the theoretical sciences.

> . . . it is not true that prudence exercises authority over wisdom or the nobler part of our intellectual being any more than the art of medicine has authority over health. The doctor's business is not to take our health into his hands but to give it a chance. Accordingly his orders are not given *to* but *for* health. To use another illustration, it would be like saying that political science is sovereign over the gods, because it issues regulations about everything in the *polis,* including what is due to them.[19]

The formation of the political association is linked by Aristotle with the human tendency to seek *friendship.* Friendship for Aristotle is viewed in a somewhat utilitarian light; we seek friends for either pleasure or profit to ourselves; an enlightened egotism is an integral part of the process. But friendship can result in *homonoia* (likemindedness, unanimity or concord). This has a bearing on politics; 'concord is friendship between the citizens of a state, its province being the interests and concerns of life'.[20] Here too the conception of a common interest is brought in, achieved possibly by a dovetailing of individual interests: 'We say there is concord in a state when the citizens agree about their interests, adopt a policy unanimously and proceed to carry it out.'[21] Following this line of thought, subordinate groupings are regarded by Aristotle as parts of the *polis*. This combining of less matured parts to form a more developed whole is well in keeping with Aristotle's general teleological principles. Justice as well as utility is operative in the process; like Plato in the *Republic*, Aristotle sees an analogy between *polis* life and family life and traces resemblances between the ways families and states may be run, according to whether they are monarchical, aristocratic or timocratic, with their perversions (tyranny, oligarchy and democracy respectively, democracy being the least bad of the perversions – we may compare here a somewhat similar attitude of Plato in the *Statesman;* he too is relatively favourable towards democracy in his distinction between lawful and lawless types of it; lawful democracy is the worst of good types of government but the best of bad types). Degrees of friendship among citizens are even held by Aristotle to be in proportion to the various types of regime. Thus the social atmosphere of a tyranny allows no chance of real friendship between citizens, for the basis of concord is lacking there.

The emphasis on friendship as the cement of human life raises the question of its relationship to the ideal of contemplation which Aristotle had regarded as superior in the *Protrepticus*. In Book IX Aristotle appears to be arguing that no man, even the best, can be self-sufficient. This is put in the strongest terms: 'Surely there is something strange in representing the man of perfect blessedness as a solitary or a recluse. Nobody would deliberately choose to have all the good things in the world, if there was a condition that he was to have them all by himself. Man is a social animal, and the need for company is in his blood.'[22] 'The solitary man has a hard time of it. It is not easy to keep up a continuous activity by oneself; in the company of others and in relation to others it is not so difficult. Consequently the activity of the good man, which is pleasurable in itself, will be less discontinuous if he has friends about him.'[23]

In Book X, on the other hand, Aristotle cites as proof of the superiority of the purely contemplative life of the philosopher the fact that it is self-sufficient. He contrasts the pleasure produced by contemplation, which has no end beyond itself, which that produced by 'political and military activities', the highest of non-philosophical pursuits; these, argues Aristotle are 'not chosen for their own sake but with a view to some remoter end', and 'are incompatible with leisure'.[24] The emphasis on leisure, by which the Greeks understood emancipation from the ordinary cares of life is not for the purpose of frivolous enjoyment, but for the pursuit of the good life. Here Aristotle seems to be presenting the life of pure contemplation alone as providing the leisure for realising full human potentialities. The conception enters the mystical field in a striking passage where Aristotle admits that his contemplative ideal is beyond strictly human attainment but must none the less be striven for by the help of the particle of divine life within each human:

> We ought not to listen to those who counsel us 'O man, think as man should' and 'O mortal, remember your mortality'. Rather ought we, so far as in us lies, to put on immortality and to leave nothing unattempted in the effort to live in conformity with the highest thing with us. Small in bulk it may be, yet in power and preciousness it transcends all the rest. We may in fact believe that this is the true self of the individual, being the sovereign and better part of him.[25]

We seem to be back at the dualism of the *Protrepticus*, with its sharp separation of soul and body. This also seems to be reflected in the subsequent passage, where Aristotle clearly subordinates the moral to the intellectual virtues, on the ground that the gods practice the latter but hardly the former, which depend on a relatively imperfect framework of life. Aristotle admits that the philosopher cannot, as a human being, detach himself from all dependence on his social environment: 'Human nature is not equal to such intense intellectual effort, if it must rely entirely on its own resources. The thinker must have a sufficiency of health and food and whatever else is necessary to keep him going.'[26] So social arrangements are in the last resort secondary, even though essential, to the production of happiness for the contemplative.

The approach to elitism in this theory is heightened by the pessimism which Aristotle shows when assessing the likelihood of the acceptance of reason's dictates by the majority of people unless they are compelled to do so by coercion.[27]

> It is the nature of the many to yield to the suggestions of fear rather than honour, and to abstain from evil not because of the disgrace but the penalties entailed by not abstaining. Living under the dictates of passion, they chase the pleasures fit for such natures and

the means of gratifying them, and they shun the pains which are the opposite of those pleasures. But the honourable and the truly delightful – of that they have no conception, having never trusted genuine pleasure. What theory, what homily can ever reform people like that?[28] . . . people are by and large readier to submit to punishment and compulsion than moved by arguments and ideals.[29]

Political authority must thus accept as one of its main tasks the forcible inculcation of ethical behaviour in those incapable of achieving it for themselves. Aristotle criticises existing Greek political governments, apart from Sparta, for shirking this responsibility and leaving too much to individual discretion in ethical matters: 'Every man does as he likes with his life in the manner of the Cyclops in Homer, "laying down the law for children and wife".'[30] One of Aristotle's purposes in approaching the scientific study of politics is to provide the well-disposed private citizen with a yardstick for the conduct of life which should ideally be provided by the *polis* itself, but in practice is not. The Sophists are no help, Aristotle decides; their emphasis on rhetoric and their limitation of political science in effect to comparative study of existing constitutions is a distortion which Aristotle proposes to remedy by a return to first principles. Aristotle writes very much as an embittered critic of existing society.

It is worth registering the ambiguity in Aristotle's attitude to political activity and its origins. On the one hand his emphasis on its foundation in friendship, co-operation and *homonoia,* would suggest a more optimistic assessment of the reason and well-disposed ethical disposition of those who came together to become citizens of the political associations. On the other hand the assertion that human rational activity can only be fully realised in a philosophical few who are above the political process inevitably leads to a disposition to downgrade politics in effect to an instrument of control of the incurable perversity of the irrational many. The ambiguity is clearly a more elaborate statement of the basic problem of the *Protrepticus* and for that matter of Platonism. It is not a matter of a tension created by Aristotle's moving away from Platonism; it is that both Aristotle and Plato share in a common tension produced by the Greek inability to reach a final solution of the problem raised by the relationship of the contemplative philosopher to the practical life of society. This internal dialogue which Aristotle inherited from Plato and translated into the context of his own specific philosophical system continues in full strength as we move from the *Ethics* to the *Politics.*

We may sum up the position at this point by saying that the conclusion of the *Ethics* appears to leave Aristotle asserting the existence of three different classes of people, as far as ethical and moral decisions are concerned:

(1) the pure philosopher, who possesses *sophia* (wisdom);
(2) the enlightened practical man who possesses *phronesis* (practical ethical insight);
(3) the mass of the unenlightened who possess neither and who therefore have to be submitted to legal coercion.

It is clear that the type (2) is the class of primary importance in politics; the philosopher is above political deliberation and choice and the masses are below it. There may be a shade of this threefold meaning in Aristotle's famous remark in *Politics,* Book I (usually and probably legitimately taken as primarily having a more general sense): 'The man who is isolated – who is unable to share in the benefits of political association, or has no need to share because he is already self-sufficient – is no part of the *polis* and must therefore be either a beast or a god.'[31] Since political science has already been defined as the direction of the community towards achieving ethical goodness, the paramount position of the man of *phronesis* is evident; Aristotle implies clearly that the whole subsequent examination of the structure of politics is written for the benefit of this enlightened practical man; in present circumstances of corruption in most states, Aristotle holds, this may well mean that the man of *phronesis* must apply his political knowledge to the limited community of his household and family. This is probably why Aristotle starts the *Politics* with an examination of the household from various aspects; he intends to elucidate for his prospective pupil, the man of *phronesis,* the similarities and differences between the 'political' and 'economic' spheres (using these in the Greeks' and Aristotle's own technical sense – conduct of public social affairs and the conduct of private household affairs respectively). The man of *phronesis* has to take responsible decisions in both spheres; in this he occupies a unique position in the social order.

Aristotle's examination starts from the premiss that the cell from which the *polis* is formed must be the family. In both communities a ruler–subject relationship is inevitable; some must govern and others must obey. It is this sense that Aristotle understands the male–female relationship in the family unit and the master–slave relationship with the household. The office of kingship, arising out of the rule of one leader over a combination of families in a clan system, is for Aristotle the bridge between political and economic fields. Modern research on early Greek history tends to substantiate Aristotle's view of this historical function of kingship, and would make the further suggestion that the progressively more complex growth of the *polis* made kingship superfluous and finally eliminated it in most Greek communities.

This examination of the nature of the household leads Aristotle to broach the question of slavery. It is clear that the validity of the institution was being questioned in Aristotle's own time, and that Aristotle rejected the contentions of the 'liberals' in this matter. His rejection is based on the argument of the natural character of slavery, some men being destined by natural endowment to supplement the lack of reason in others for the good of the less fortunately endowed. Aristotle clearly has in mind the desirability of rule by the man of *phronesis* over those who have not his insight. This is carried to the extent of postulating rather unconvincing physical differences between the two types; Aristotle himself confesses the breakdown of his scheme here by admitting that physical and intellectual character does not always correspond. This attempt to correlate physical and mental characteristics had already been initiated in various parts of the *Ethics*. Aristotle rejects the idea of a purely *legal* as distinct from natural slavery, i.e. the fixing of the slave status as a result of purely conventional circumstances such as war against fellow-Greeks (barbarians do not count). Greek opinion had already moved in this direction – the enslavement of fellow-citizens in Athens had been forbidden as long ago as the time of Solon (early sixth century) and in Aristotle's own time legislation by the Athenian statesman Lycurgus (*c.* 330 BC), forbade the enslavement of freemen from any state who had been captured in war. We know that there was a certain connection between Aristotle and Lycurgus.

Within these limits Aristotle asserts unlimited control of the slave by his master. This control rests on a qualitative superiority; the master stands to the slave in the same relationship as soul to body and this legitimates the master's control. Aristotle does not hesitate to depict the slave as the instrument of the master, his property, to be used for his rational purposes – the soul-body relationship is in the background again.

Aristotle's treatment of slavery is clearly completely out of harmony with modern humane thought on the matter, and it is useless to pretend otherwise. What we are concerned with here, however, is to ask how Aristotle's views on the subject fit into the framework of his general conceptions of ethics and politics and to practical pattern of slavery in his own time.

Slavery as a Greek institution in Aristotle's time had already passed through a number of historical changes. In the archaic period the distinction between slave and free (at least freemen belonging to the lower classes) was more shadowy than it became in the classical period (after the Persian Wars). In the Homeric world the slave is clearly the living property of the master, usually acquired by capture in war. But the slave seems to have been accepted as an integral part of the family unit, enjoying not only the protection but even sometimes the friendship and affection of those within it. An example from the *Odyssey* would be the bonds of affection linking Odysseus and his faithful swinehead Eumaeus. It is significant that in this earlier period the same Greek word is used to describe both a slave and a free servant – later usage employed a special word to describe a slave. Homer does not use the word in the masculine gender at all and in the feminine only twice in the whole of his works. Clearly the basic relationship at the early stage was not between slave and free, but between a master or lord and those who worked for him, whether technically slaves or not. In the first half of the seventh century Hesiod takes it for granted that the small farmer, besides his essential requirements of a house, a wife and draught animals, should also enjoy the services of permanent employees who seem to be slaves, as distinct from the hired labourers whom he uses at harvest times. The slaves are members of his household, with whom he feels a close personal bond.

This early purely household stage of slavery was changed by the commercial and mercantile economic revolution of the seventh century onwards. The wartime expansion of this period, the foundation of colonies abroad, the opening up of markets for products such as pottery and olives in return for the basic cereals and foodstuffs of which Greece was in such short supply, led to the growth of relatively large commercial complexes to take advantage of the new opportunities. This produced a need for a cheap labour force, which was met by the traffic in slaves from barbarian lands. The increase in the number of slaves used now, not so much by the private household unit as by the more bigger, impersonal and exacting proto-capitalist commercial and industrial enterprises for production of goods for a mass market, meant that the slaves became more sharply differentiated as a class and on the whole worse treated. In Athens, ironically enough, the stratification of slavery as an institution was carried to its climax by the democracy with its interest in overseas commercial and manufacturing expansion, in which the free citizens jealously emphasised their privileges against the slave population, almost exclusively non-Athenian.

It would not be true to imply that the use of slaves in the private household died out in the later period. Aristotle himself, who points out that too many slaves are difficult to organise efficiently, nevertheless had nine slaves, not including their children.

A. H. M. Jones, on the other hand, in his more recent classic, *Athenian Democracy*, asserts that it is unlikely that any slaves at all were owned by two-thirds to three-quarters of the citizen population. Whichever is right, it seems clear that corporative enterprises rather than private individuals and families had by the fifth century become the chief users of slaves.[32]

Among these corporate slaveowners was the Athenian *polis* itself, which relied on the use of slaves for a surprising range of permanent civic functions, including whatever approximated to a civil service or police force. The police function was carried out by Scythian archers; we have some vivid pictures of them rounding up citizen idlers from the market place and shopping centre on days of public assembly and driving them bodily towards the Pnyx, the open-air place of meeting for Athenian democracy, where these defaulting freemen should be doing their duty debating or voting. In the Pnyx itself a body of more highly educated slaves who were in permanent charge of the city's accounts and records sat discreetly hidden behind the president's rostrum and passed him up minutes for his guidance from time to time. These slaves were in fact almost permanent under-secretaries. We find other slaves looking after banks or commercial firms for their masters; one of them in the fourth century, Pasion, even manages to go into business on his own account and becomes a millionaire and, finding this extreme example too paradoxical even by contemporary standards, Athens gives him his freedom.[33]

Other slaves of the state were not so fortunate. Those who worked at the silver mines at Laurium, owned by the city, did so in conditions of grinding misery; one Marxist historian of ancient Greece, George Thomson, has argued (*Studies in Ancient Greek Society*, Vol. II) that Laurium was the inspiration for the harrowing imagery of the Cave in Plato's *Republic*. At one point in the Peloponnesian War, 22,000 slaves from Athens took the chance of deserting to the Spartans, themselves with a rather bad reputation for the treatment of their own helots. The industrial concerns, pottery, metalworking, arms manufacturing, and so on, worked chiefly on slave labour hired from a few big slaveowners. The statesman Nicias is hiring out 1,000 slaves in the late fifth century, and Xenophon in the early fourth advocates what amounts to a nationalisation of existing slave labour by compulsory purchase and profitable hiring out. Even what we can call the entertainment industry (flute-girls, dancers, acrobats and the like) was provided almost entirely from a hired-out slave population. On occasion a slave of this sort might even live by himself in conditions of only legal subjection to his master. He would be required to contribute the financial profit made by his labour to his master, though sometimes he was allowed to retain a portion of it, large or small according to the master's will.

It is thus clear that by Aristotle's time there were two main types of slavery, one (the household and domestic type) older but shrinking in importance; the other (the type absorbed by the new corporative economic enterprises) more recent but by now comprising the much greater part of the slave population. The striking feature of Aristotle's treatment of the subject is that it is the first type of slavery only which appears to take into account. This cannot be by accident; the omission is obviously deliberate. Why?

We may suggest that Aristotle is arguing by implication that the only legitimate type of slavery is that which finds its framework in the natural focus of the household. This may be the real reason for his insistence on the natural character of slavery as an institution, coupled with his rejection of the idea that the basis of slavery is merely superior force. Aristotle is in fact harking back to the older idea of the slave as a member of the family group, the sort of relationship depicted by Homer and Hesiod. To this oldfashioned conservative picture he even adds a touch of philosophical liberalising by taking up the hint dropped in the *Ethics* of a possibility of real friendship and communion of minds between master and slave:

A wrong exercise of his rule by a master is a thing which is disadvantageous for both master and slave. The part and the whole, like the body and the soul, have an identical interest; and the slave is a part of the master, in the sense of being a living but separate part of his body. There is thus a community of interest, and a relation of friendship, between master and slave, when both of them naturally merit the position in which they stand. But the reverse is true when matters are otherwise and slavery rests merely on legal sanction and superior power.[34]

These passages approach a conception of voluntary acceptance of slave status by an individual for his own good within the framework of a hierarchically functioning system. Aristotle's support of this type of slave institutional status, as well as his opposition to the industrial and corporate slavery of more recent times, is dictated by his overarching conception, which we saw at the end of the *Ethics*, of society as a direction towards the common good of those who are not able to attain this good of their own volition by those who are possessed of the know-how (*phronesis*) to do so. It is thus clear that Aristotle is of the opinion that the necessary control of society by the man of *phronesis* has been frustrated by the development of slavery other than as a household unit, in which a minimum of personal relationship between master and slave can be preserved.

Aristotle shows a similarly conservative or liberal standpoint (paradoxically his attitude partakes of both) when he turns to considering the broader pattern of the economic background as a whole. His account of the origin of the use of money as the primary medium of exchange is remarkably acute and historically accurate, as far as Greek society is concerned. Aristotle does not wish to put the clock back to a primitive type of society with barter as its exchange medium; but he does level an attack on what he calls the abuse of *chrematistic*, the acquisition of money for its own sake over and above the complete satisfaction of natural needs. He cites retail trade and, still more, usury (though without going into much detail) as examples of the unnatural application of the chrematistic art. In each case the balance of society is upset by an undue desire for individual gain – the besetting sin, Aristotle seems to imply, of the commercial way of life of which democratic Athens was the archetype.

We thus see that for Aristotle correct life within the household and family group at least embodies a strict and yet rational hierarchical system, in which the true master, the possessor of *phronesis*, will be the leader and guide. Following this hierarchical argument, Aristotle parts company with Plato in his conception of moral virtue (*arete*). Plato, particularly in the *Meno*, had argued for a single quality of moral virtue, a unified quality of goodness, inherent in every human being as such; it may be significant that Plato uses the character of a slave boy in this dialogue to demonstrate his point; the boy is led by Socrates to discover his potentiality of reason by solving a previously unknown geometrical problem. Aristotle holds that instead of one all-embracing moral virtue in the Platonic style there are in reality a number of moral virtues, varying according to the status of each particular type of person in the hierarchical social ladder. The moral virtue of the master must be different from that of the salve, that of the male from that of the female, that of the adult from that of the child, and so on.

The relevance of this theory of social differentiation and elitism to spheres broader than that of the family group is shown by Aristotle's concluding remarks in Book I, where he makes a deliberate link between household and political community by stating that the specific virtues of women and children can only be discussed in the framework of political relationships, as they contribute to the collective virtue of the *polis*. Aristotle nowhere fulfils this promise, but this is perhaps not so important as the motive behind it – the confession that the rules applicable to the household are to apply to the *polis* also. We would expect this from the general character of Aristotle's philosophy of development in general, but it would seem that we also have here to take into consideration Aristotle's objective of implementing the supremacy of the rule of *phronesis* in politics. From the evidence of this first book of the *Politics*, we can see that in practice this will mean a challenge from a point of view both rationalist and conservative to elements in contemporary society, particularly stemming from the ethics of profit-making economic activity, which Aristotle holds to be inimical to a correct orientation of individual and *polis*. We may suggest that the inference from Book I is that Aristotle's approach to politics will be no purely detached and scientifically dispassionate one, but will in fact be primarily an assertion of a programme. In Book I this intention can be detected fairly obviously, but we shall now have to inquire if the same applies to the more apparently objective central books.

Book III is usually and rightly regarded as the central section of the *Politics*, in which the general structural themes of the work are laid down. For some scholars indeed it would form the beginning of Aristotle's whole inquiry. Here Aristotle explores again the question which has fascinated him in the *Ethics* – the relationship between moral virtue and civic activity; here however he takes the argument a stage further by linking it to the observable structure and development of different existing forms of political regime.

Before analysing the different stages of his argument, we have to recognise that there is one long section of Book III which does not seem to dovetail very easily into the context of the rest of the book. This is the discussion of kingship, from the end of 1284 b (Barker, p. 137) to 1288 a (Barker, p. 150), which would logically belong to the discussion of the various types of constitution in Book IV. I am suggesting that this section is not an integral part of the argument but has found its way into the text at this point because of a superficial similarity between its discussion of kingship and Aristotle's discussion of the possibility of kingly rule by one man or group of men in the main body of the book. I shall try to suggest reasons for this belief when we have discussed the argument of the main portion of the book.

One of the things which strikes us about Aristotle's whole argument throughout the book is its somewhat tentative and erratic nature. He takes up one opinion after the other, points out its advantages and disadvantages, digresses frequently and does not really in the end answer his initial question (itself expressed in mock-despairing even ironical terms at the start of the book): 'Whatever on earth is the polis?' conveys the nuance of the Greek text better than our usual rather wooden English rendering: 'What is the state' or 'What is the nature of the polis?' The tone of the question, as well as the whole subsequent discussion, suggests that Aristotle is not broaching an inquiry to establish the general definition of the *polis* in the abstract. He is rather setting about elucidating the bewildering variety of features which is presented by the *polis* as it exists. His own technique of argument matches the profusion of types presented by the Greek *polis* in his day. Aristotle is here describing rather than defining; he is stating a case rather than seeking disinterested scientific precision.

Aristotle begins by arguing that the nature of the *polis* is impossible to dissociate from the social arrangement of the citizens who compose it. After rejecting definitions of a citizen based on residence and competence to engage in litigation (capacities which may be shared by slaves and aliens) Aristotle plumps for participation in legal and administrative office-holding as a more satisfactory description. Almost immediately however Aristotle seems to feel that his description is only applicable in an unqualified sense to one particular regime – democracy: 'We may thus conclude that the citizen of our definition is particularly and especially the citizen of a democracy. Citizens living under other kinds of constitution *may* possibly, but do not necessarily, correspond to the definition.'[35] It is clear that Aristotle has Athens primarily in mind in framing this only partially adequate definition. This impression is strengthened by the presence of a somewhat critical remark in which Aristotle dismisses as a quibble the view that the popular assembly in democratic cities is not to be regarded as composed of officeholders. 'It would be ridiculous to exclude from the category of officeholders those who actually hold the most sovereign position in the state';[36] this is very much in line with what we know from other sources to have been the familiar criticism of Athenian democracy by its opponents, i.e. that it subordinated law to the arbitrary will of the majority of the popular body. The same concentration on Athenian conditions is found in later references[37] to the confinement of citizenship to those of native birth on both sides; this had been established as a legal *sine qua non* at Athens under the inspiration of Pericles in 451 BC. This legislation was in sharp contrast to previous Athenian legislation on the same subject after the revolution led by Cleisthenes in 509 BC, the effective date of foundation of the full Athenian democracy. Aristotle implies that the arbitrary change in composition of the citizen body in each of these cases has no status except in the erroneous decision of the majority which decreed the change; it is not in accord with any rationally just norms. Thus it possesses no status except a purely *de facto* one, based on majority force.

The mention of force as a factor in change of regime in the *polis* as it exists in practice leads Aristotle to his fundamental contention that, as things stand, the *polis* is profoundly changed whenever its controlling regime changes. 'If a polis is a form of association, and if this form of association is an association of citizens in a polity (*politeia*) or constitution, it would seem to follow inevitably that when the constitution suffers a change in kind, and becomes a different constitution, the *polis* also will cease to be the same polis, and will also change its identity.'[38] Aristotle is glancing back here to his discussion of friendship in the *Ethics* as a personal association of like-minded persons. He follows this up here by emphasising that the political association was conditioned by the character of those composing it.

This assessment of political change by the varying ethical quality of the persons composing the *polis* leads Aristotle to the question of the relationship of fully-developed moral goodness to civic excellence. This is what is behind the question: 'Is the good man identical with the good citizen?' Aristotle decides in the negative; just as Book I has established that different functions in society call for differing types of virtue, so now the virtue of the citizen varies according to the type of regime with which he is concerned. Even his yardsticks of moral behaviour will shift with each political variation. This cannot be said of the good man, the man of *phronesis*, who, as the *Ethics* showed, pursues a consistent pattern of virtue whose guiding principles can be applied to all circumstances.

This distinction, while regarded by Aristotle as true in existing political life, is applied by him even to the case of the ideal city. Following his pessimistic estimate in the *Ethics* that most ordinary men are incapable of the rational insight necessary for complete moral virtue, he concludes that, while all citizens cannot in the nature of things be morally good in the responsible sense in which the good man himself is, they nevertheless can be good citizens, i.e. they can accept and fulfil their correct political function. Aristotle emphasises this by going back to his Book I comparison between reason and appetite, soul and body, man and wife, master and slave, and saying explicitly that 'the polis too is composed of different and unlike elements'.[39] In other words, the same standards should apply to household and *polis*.

Aristotle now draws the conclusion that in a correctly ordered *polis* the ruler requires *phronesis*; it is therefore in his case alone that the virtues of good man and good citizen are identical.

Prudence (*phronesis*) is the only form of goodness which is peculiar to the ruler. The other forms of virtue [i.e. temperance, justice and courage] must, it would seem, belong equally to rulers and subjects. The form of goodness peculiar to subjects cannot be prudence and may be defined as right opinion. The ruled may be compared to flute-makers; rulers are like flute-players who use what the flute-makers make.[40]

Aristotle's view of government here is very reminiscent of that of Plato; in particular his distinction between the *phronesis,* or ethical insight, of the rulers and the mere 'right opinion' of the subjects reminds us of the *Republic's* distinction between the knowledge of the philosopher Guardians and the opinion of the rest of the community. The flute analogy appears to indicate that the function of the subject is to supply, by conformity to the type of virtue appropriate to his status, a variety of services to the *polis* which will be used to the general benefit by the ruler, who alone possesses the ability to co-ordinate the different functions for the common good. The only real difference from Plato is that the *phronesis* of the ethically wise practical man is substituted for the philosophical knowledge which is the distinguishing feature of Plato's rulers.

It now begins to be clear that this whole discussion of moral and civic virtue has been utilised by Aristotle to make the same point as he has done in Book I, i.e. that a correctly governed *polis* can only be obtained on hierarchical social lines; the parting of the ways with the democracy of his time is obvious. This is underlined by his following assertion that ideally mechanics, i.e. the artisan and labouring classes, should be excluded from the citizen rights on the ground that their menial duties do not allow them the leisure necessary for participation in politics. One feels that Aristotle does not draw much distinction here between these 'free' labourers and the slaves themselves: 'The truth is that we cannot include as citizens all who are necessary conditions of the state's existence.'[41]

Aristotle has thus once more stated his case for the ideal supremacy of the possessor of *phronesis* in political as well as ethical decision making. He is aware however that his argument is applicable in its full extent in the sphere of the ideal only, and the account must also be taken of currently existing practice, with its greater or lesser extent of approximation to the ideal or even (in the case of what he calls 'perversions') the complete lack of approximation to it. He admits that the mere urge for survival, for clinging to life, may be a minimally valid reason for political association. From this angle the most ethically backward political unit may possess its own value. This attitude, a little difficult to reconcile with Aristotle's previous ethically rigorist argument, is indicative of the irrepressible interest in the concrete and particular which is one of Aristotle's fundamental characteristics. Even when driven hard by his quasi-Platonic wish for the control of politics by ethics, he never quite loses his interest in the variety of empirical behaviour, imperfect though it be. Life and existence itself, as he declares here, possesses its own intrinsic quality of goodness. The tension which here exists in Aristotle's thought cannot be formulated in terms of Jaeger's contrast between Platonic idealism and the 'organisation of research', but must rather be viewed as a tension between more limited and more liberal application of a single ethical ideal.

As far as politics is concerned, Aristotle sees the legitimacy or otherwise of any given system of government as being dependent upon one touchstone – the conformity of the government to the task of pursuing the common good. He takes up Plato's point in *Republic*, Book I, that the art of government, like other arts, such as medicine and gymnastics, is exercised primarily with a view to the common good of the objects of the art – the patients in medicine, those to be instructed in gymnastics and the ruled in politics. If the practitioner of any of these arts pays his *primary* attention to the personal benefit he can obtain from the art, then he is using his skill in an illegitimate manner. In the case of politics this implies that a government, whatever its complexion, can only be just if it serves the common good.

Aristotle applies this reasoning to distinguish between concrete types of legal and illegal government. Six main types can be discerned, according to him – three good and three bad. Legitimate one-man government for common good (kingship) is contrasted with tyranny – personal government for the selfish benefit of the ruler only. Aristocracy (rule of the few best men) for the community's benefit is placed over against oligarchy, in which the few rulers exploit the community. Finally Aristotle presents two types of democracy – a moderate type, or 'polity', which allows all citizens to participate in government for the common good, and a deviationist type in which the masses tyrannise for their own benefit (a situation which, as he makes clear elsewhere, prevails at Athens itself). The first two distinctions are clear enough, the latter not so clear at this stage. One might well ask for the criteria by which democratic government may be assessed as conforming or not conforming to the common good – is Aristotle searching, in the manner of Rousseau later, for some sort of abstract distinction between the 'general will' and 'the will of all'? Fortunately for clarity, Aristotle does later (in Book IV) provide some concrete constitutional details to elucidate his distinction between the two types of democracy. Without anticipating fuller discussion, we can note here that Aristotle, as will be seen later, is attempting to revive the ideal of the older type of Athenian democracy inaugurated by Solon in the early sixth century, which gave all citizens the right of election in the assembly and the right to sit in the law courts, but preserved the higher offices of state for the aristocracy. This was set aside at the end of the same century by the reforms of Cleisthenes, which threw open all offices of the *polis* to all citizens and initiated the period of full radical democracy which Plato, Aristotle and other conservative writers had come to distrust. It has been shown by modern study[42] that the appeal to go back to the Solonian constitution was a standard argument of the more conservative democrats (to call them 'oligarchs' might be a distortion) throughout the later fifth and the whole of the fourth centuries BC. Aristotle's own work, *The Athenian Constitution* (even if it is not by himself – but a member of his school), shows the same tendency to depict the history of Athens as a degeneration from the correct balance achieved by the settlement of Solon. This school of thought would comprise the people to whom Aristotle's concept of the 'polity' would be likely to appeal; they would also be those likely to share Aristotle's concern with the commercial, manufacturing and maritime expansion which were held to go hand in hand with extreme democracy.

Aristotle's conviction that the economic revolution had played a large share in the deterioration of Greek political life is again illustrated by his adoption of the criterion of distribution of economic power to distinguish between the different types of *bad* regimes – among the good types, wealth, though it has its importance, is placed well after ethical merit as a criterion of differentiation. Thus oligarchy, despite its name, is defined by Aristotle as a political regime manipulated for the benefit of the wealthy; democracy, again despite its name, is government in the interests of the poor. The fact that by the nature of things the rich are usually few and the poor many is beside the point. What matters is the economic motivating force behind each of these types of government.

Aristotle holds that both types of bad government prove their weakness by their incorrect conceptions of justice. (It is to be noted that he misses out any consideration of tyranny at all, as being self-evidently bad and as making no attempt whatever to realise political justice.) Democracy takes justice to mean equality pure and simple, conferred by free birth; oligarchy realises the inadequacy of this but supposes that inequality is a matter of greater or lesser degrees of economic wealth. Aristotle argues that both overlook the

77

quality of ethical development which the political association, like friendship, has as its true objective.

The corporate quality of politics which Aristotle thus emphasises leads him to put forward with an objectivity which might seem remarkable the case for democracy. He argues that the mass of people do possess in their collective capacity qualities of virtue and even *phronesis* which may enable them on occasion to have a better judgement than the few of higher intelligence; he cites the practice of allowing music and poetry to be assessed by majority popular approval. Aristotle is here quite at loggerheads with Plato, who would allow no merit at all in popular judgement: in the *Republic* we have a vivid picture of the distate inspired in Plato the aristocrat by popular meetings:

> When they sit together, wedged in their crowds, in the political assemblies, the law courts, the theatres and any other public gatherings, censuring or applauding words and actions with their vociferous shouts, tasteless alike in their blame and praise, so that the very stones round the arena in which they have assembled echo to their cries and multiply the appalling noise.[43]

Nor did Plato have any use for the popular judgement on aesthetic performances, the 'theatocracy', as he bitterly names it in the *Laws*, which Aristotle is here inclined to approve.

On closer examination it is clear that Aristotle's praise of democracy here is intended to apply only to the more moderate, 'legitimate' type of it. This is obvious from Aristotle's stipulation, here with the explicit citation of Solon, that the mass of ordinary citizens should be allowed the right of election to deliberative and judicial functions, but not the right of individual office holding. This is because Aristotle is following his immediately previous argument of the *collective* nature of popular political capacity by the conclusion that this capacity is forfeited when individual members of the populace act singly. Critical judgement of political possibilities rather than initiation of them is where Aristotle sees the strength of the rank and file of citizens to lie; the specialist, as he further points out, is not necessarily the best judge of his own work. It is the man who lives in a house rather than the man who builds it who must be the final judge of its soundness; the man who eats a dinner has the last word as against the cook. Aristotle's defence of democracy, even though of a qualified form of democracy, has considerable power and has exercised a proportionate influence in subsequent ages. Modern representative democracy would seem in some ways to correspond to Aristotle's conviction that criticism and assessment rather than instruction and elaboration of policies is the correct key to the role of most citizens in the democratic process.

Again in keeping with the older moderate democratic Athenian tradition, Aristotle emphasises the all-important role of law in maintaining civic stability. Law is. dependent on justice; Aristotle refers back to his definition of justice in the *Ethics*. Here he had distinguished between distributive and rectificatory justice. The former, which is more closely connected by him with political activity proper, is described by Barker[44] as 'the justice shown by the whole state in distributing offices, honours and other benefits among its members'. The distribution is carried out in proportion to the varying and therefore unequal merits of the different recipients. Aristotle holds that all depends for each *polis* on the criterion by which this distributive justice is implemented. His own view is of course that ethical virtues are as logical criteria as wealth and free birth for the exercise of citizenship. In the case of the ideal *polis* the citizen body must be composed of ' . . . those who are able and willing to rule and be ruled with a view to attaining a way of life according to goodness'.[45]

It is thus only in the ideal *polis* that those men who possess *phronesis* in its full sense will be able to devote themselves with complete effectiveness to the service of the community. In other political bodies the man of *phronesis* will find himself the odd man out and will probably suffer accordingly. This pessimistic estimate is at the back of Aristotle's rather obscure remarks about the outstanding individual or group of individuals who are

> so pre-eminently superior in goodness that there can be no comparison between the goodness and political capacity which he shows (or several show, when there is more than one) and what is shown by the rest, such a person, or such persons, can no longer be treated as part of the state. Being so greatly superior to others in goodness and political capacity, they will suffer injustice if they are treated as worthy only of an equal share; for a person of this order may very well be like a god among men.[46]

Hans Kelsen, in an interesting article,[47] has suggested that this and other similar passages in Book III are to be seen as an *apologia* for Macedonian supremacy over Greece and particularly as support for the claim of divine kingship which Alexander the Great was making at the time Aristotle was writing. As against this one must cite the comparative absence of reference to Alexander's new-style monarchy in the *Politics* as a whole, which, as has often been mentioned, confines its attention exclusively to the problems of the city-state and, in this particular passage, the readiness to contemplate the likelihood of a plurality of such gifted individuals – surely an impossible remark if Alexander and his type of monarchy are specifically in mind. It seems more plausible to interpret this passage as one more assertion of the ideal desirability of political control by men qualified with ethical insight (*phronesis*) as Aristotle sees it, together with a gloomy estimate of the feasibility of realising such control in present conditions. Aristotle envisages in fact that the average *polis* would exclude such men from its organisation as being literally too good for it. There is a throw-back to the Platonic position that the philosopher need no law when Aristotle declares: 'There can be no law which runs against men who are utterly superior to others. They are a law in themselves.'[48] Aristotle suggests, perhaps with a touch of irony, that ostracism had been the Athenian way of ridding the *polis* of such unabsorbable elements; but he also quotes instances from the other forms of perverted regime (as well as from Persia, which is outside the scheme altogether) to show that the man of *phronesis* is also unwelcome in oligarchies and tyrannies. Aristotle finishes the section by arguing that the man of *phronesis* should ideally be permanently king in his community.

The next section of Book III[49] deals with kingship as an actual form of constitution and does not, I think, have any necessary connection with the previous discussion about the citizen of outstanding merit. It may owe its place here in the final arrangement of the Aristotelean corpus to a superficial similarity with the preceding section. The chief point of interest in the section is the discussion of the relationship of monarchy to law and an incidental but important description of the nature of law.

During the fourth century a number of thinkers in the Greek world were canvassing the possibility of a monarchy of some kind as an answer to the perennial and crippling divisions within each *polis* and within Greece as a whole. Some of these thinkers, like Xenophon, argued that the ideal king they were looking for would willingly obey the laws of his community; this would be what would differentiate him from a tyrant. Plato however in the *Republic* and still more in the *Statesman* was to argue that the wise ruler should be unfettered by the law; Aristotle seems to echo this in the passage mentioned earlier. In the present section, however, he seems to argue on different lines (another point in favour of regarding this section as originally separate, with a more integral connection with Book IV). Aristotle here holds that even the best and most reasonable of men is subject to the distorting influence of passion on occasion, whereas 'Law contains no element of passion'[50] and is hence superior. Aristotle resolves the problem by providing for the government a wide scope of discretionary power in cases where the letter of the law is ambiguous or unfair in its operation. He calls on his theory of Ἐρισικεια (equity),[51] a concept unused by Plato, but which Aristotle was to make an essential element of future European legal philosophy. Law need not be, as Plato at one stage was inclined to think, a hindrance to unfettered rationality; in fact Aristotle defines it as 'Reason free from all passion'.[52]

Aristotle expresses a decided preference for unwritten compared with written law:

> . . . to seek for justice is to seek for a neutral authority; and law is a neutral authority. But laws resting on unwritten custom are even more sovereign, and concerned with issues of still more sovereign importance, than written laws; and this suggests that, even if the rule of a man be safer than the rule of written law, it need not therefore be safer than the rule of unwritten law.[53]

This corresponds to the approach taken in the *Ethics*, where justice is described as 'divided into written and unwritten';[54] Aristotle takes this to be parallel to two types of friendship, one moral, the other legal. Athenian legal philosophy knew of a distinction between unwritten and written law; the former was supposed to partake of a more venerable and axiomatic character than the latter, and corresponded somewhat to the concept of 'fundamental laws' in some modern legal systems, i.e. principles on which the specific details of legislation depend. In Athens in Aristotle's time there was even provision made for the introduction of proceedings against measures, even when taken by a majority, which were suspected of contravening these fundamental laws.

The conception of unwritten laws of Athens and other Greek cities goes back to ancient conceptions of communal laws as being directly instituted by the gods – the older Greek word for law, *thesmos*, expresses this conviction; its comes from a verb meaning 'to establish permanently'. Thus the laws were sacred and immutable, because divinely instituted. The economic and social changes in Greek society between 700 and 500 BC led to a less static conception of law and it is significant that in Athens a new word, *nomos*, completely replaces *thesmos* round about 500. It has been very plausibly suggested[55] that this change in terminology was a direct result of the revolution led by Cleisthenes about 509, which transformed the Athenian constitution from an aristocratic to a democratic one. *Nomos* carried with it a connotation of self-conscious and deliberate law making, which reflected the new democracy's insistence on the right of the people to frame the laws under which it would live.

In the light of what we have seen of Aristotle's suspicion of unrestricted democracy, we can perhaps suggest the real point behind his insistence on the superiority of unwritten law. He wishes to avoid the fault (of which Athenian democracy was often accused) of making law a purely pragmatic instrument of the people's will; for Aristotle, as for Plato, it must be more than this; it must embody unchanging principles of right conduct which must ideally be in control of all legislative activity. Aristotle revives the old conception of *thesmos* but rationalises it.

It is clear that Aristotle is on the way to what later philosophies were to formulate more precisely as the theory of natural law. In the *Rhetoric* Aristotle even appears to approach an explicit definition of this when he talks of a distinction between 'universal law' and 'particular law'. 'By particular law I mean that *written* law which regulates the life of a specific political community; by universal law, all those *unwritten* principles which are supposed to be acknowledged everywhere.'[56] Here we apparently have a straightforward contrast between written *positive* law (as Aquinas would call it) and *unwritten* natural law. Aristotle somewhat confuses the issue however by going on to say that particular law itself is partly written and partly unwritten; it is clear that he is in fact envisaging a vague outline of what amounts to a threefold division of law: (1) the lowest section – the specific legal enactments of particular communities, set forth in definite explicit statutes; (2) the principles or 'fundamental' laws of the community behind these statutes; (3) the 'universal law', described by him here as the 'law of nature', which stands behind both the other forms and gives them their validity. 'For there really exists, as all of us in some measure divine, a natural form of the just and unjust which is common to all men, even when there is no community or covenant to bind them to one another.'[57] The mediating character of the (2) form of law is evident and is strongly reminiscent of the same midway position occupied by the man of *phronesis* in Aristotle's system. In each case we have a process of implementation of abstract immutable principles in concrete fluctuating circumstances by a mediating factor which has characteristics from each of the contrasting worlds of abstract truth and concrete particulars.

Another element in Aristotle's direct statement 'Universal law is the law of nature' may be his desire to overcome the antithesis made by many Sophistic thinkers of the fifth and fourth centuries BC between law and nature (the famous '*nomos-physis*' controversy); for Aristotle there is in fact no conflict between the two concepts; the system of nature itself is one of order through law and his picture of social and political life is dominated by this belief.

The emphasis on justice in the *Ethics*, *Rhetoric* and *Politics* can hardly be dissociated from Aristotle's knowledge of current practice in the law courts of Athens; he is aware that jury service is a function which his man of *phronesis*, like other citizens, will inevitably be called on to perform. Aristotle is trying to provide him with the rules which will enable him to carry out his duties in accordance with the ethical norms which should regulate all his conduct. These rules are not identical with ethical norms, though they may be inspired by them. Thus, as one commentator has put it: 'A rule which is conventional in this sense may express a principle which is natural, e.g. as the rule of the road embodies the principle that human life should not be needlessly endangered.'[58] Or, as Aristotle himself expresses it in the *Ethics*: ' . . . The same is true of purely man-made laws. They are not the same everywhere, because forms of government are not the same. This does not alter the fact that there is only one natural form of government, namely, that which is best.'[59] This characteristic combination of relativism with a normative standard is the key to the approach to the study of actually existing constitutions in Books IV–VI of the *Politics*.

Notes Chapter IV

1 The idea that a separate science of ethics can be found in Aristotle's writings has been ably disproved by S. Cashdollar, 'Aristotle's politics of morals', *Journal of the History of Philosophy*, XI (1973), pp. 145–60.
2 Though in Chapter VI we shall discuss an important context in which the *Eudemian Ethics* is a better guide to Aristotle's meaning.
3 In the present chapter the phrase 'the Ethics' is always to be understood to refer to the *Nicomachean Ethics*.
4 I, ii, 1904 b (translation by J. A. K. Thomson, *The Ethics of Aristotle*, Penguin Classics, 1955, p. 27). All subsequent quotations from the *Nicomachean Ethics* will be made from this translation.
5 ibid.
6 I, iii, 1095 a, Thomson, p. 28.
7 I, vii, 1097 b, Thomson, p. 37.
8 I, ix, 1099 b, Thomson, p. 44.
9 I, viii, 1102 a, Thomson, p. 51.
10 ibid.
11 II, i, 1103 b, Thomson, p. 56.
12 III, iii, 113 a, Thomson, p. 87.

13 III, iii, 1112 a, Thomson, p. 185.

14 ibid., 1112 b, Thomson, p. 86.

15 ibid.

16 VI, vii, 1141 a, Thomson, p. 179. I have ventured to substitute 'universe' for Thomson's 'world' as a rendering of the Greek *cosmos*, as it would seem to me that this expresses the original more precisely.

17 VI, vii, 1141 b, Thomson, p. 180.

18 VI, viii, 1141 b, Thomson, p. 181.

19 VI, xiii, 1145 a, Thomson, pp. 191–92.

20 IX, vi, 1167 b, Thomson, p. 271.

21 ibid., 1167 a, Thomson, p. 270.

22 IX, ix, 1169 b, Thomson, p. 277.

23 ibid., 1170 a, Thomson, p. 278.

24 X, vii, 1177 b, Thomson, p. 304.

25 ibid., 1178 a, Thomson, p. 305.

26 X, viii, 1179 a, Thomson, p. 308.

27 It is significant that Aristotle elsewhere points out that the very word *akolasia* (incontinence') has as its literal meaning 'the condition which results from not being chastised' and refers to the naughtiness of children, which has a certain resemblance to the wantonness of their elders (III, xii, 1119 b, Thomson, p. 107).

28 X, ix, 1179 b, Thomson, p. 310.

29 ibid., 1190 b, Thomson, p. 311.

30 ibid., 1180 a, Thomson, p. 312.

31 *Politics,* I, xiv, 1253 a (translation by E. Barker, *The Politics of Aristotle,* Oxford, 1946). All quotations from the *Politics* will be made from this translation.

32 For good surveys of the historical development of slavery, see M. Pohlenz, *Freedom and Life in Greek Thought* (Dordrecht, 1966); H. Michell, *The Economics of Ancient Greece* (2nd edn, New York, 1963); A. French, *The Growth of the Athenian Economy* (London, 1964); and A. H. M. Jones, *Athenian Democracy* (Oxford, 1957). M. I. Finley has edited a collection of important recent essays in *Slavery in Classical Antiquity* (Cambridge and New York, 1968).

33 We also find slaves being employed as overseers of other slaves. Aristotle himself remarks: 'Those who are in a position to escape from being troubled by it delegate the management of slaves to a steward, and spend on politics or philosophy the time they are thus able to save' (*Politics,* I, vii, 1255 b, Barker, p. 18).

34 *Politics,* I, vi, 1255 b, Barker, pp. 16–17.

35 III, i, 1275 b, Barker, p. 95.

36 ibid., 1275 a, Barker, p. 94.

37 III, ii, 1275 b and 1276 a, Barker, pp. 96–7.

38 III, iii, 1276 b, Barker, p. 99.

39 III, iv, 1277 a, Barker, p. 102.

40 III, iv, 1277 b, Barker, p. 106.

41 III, v, 1278 a, Barker, p. 108.

42 See especially A. Fuks, *The Ancestral Constitution: Four studies in Athenian party politics at the end of the fifth century BC* (London, 1953; repr. Westport, Connecticut, 1971 and 1975).

43 *Republic,* 492 b–c.

44 Appendix II, p. 363.

45 *Politics,* III, xiii, 1284 a, Barker, p. 134.
46 ibid., Barker, pp. 134–5.
47 H. Kelsen, 'The philosophy of Aristotle and the Hellenic-Macedonian policy', *Ethics,* 48 (October 1937) (repr. in W. Ebenstein, ed., *Political Thought in Perspective,* New York, 1957, pp. 56–86).
48 *Politics,* III, xiii, 1284 a, Barker, p. 135.
49 xiv–xvii, 1284 b – 1288 a, Barker, pp. 137–51.
50 ibid., xv, 1286 a, Barker, p. 141.
51 For fuller discussion of justice, law and equity, see Barker, *Politics,* Appendix II, pp. 363–72, and M. Hamburger, *Morals and Law: The growth of Aristotle's legal theory* (New Haven, 1951) pp. 64–5, 89–105.
52 *Politics,* III, xvi, 1287 a, Barker, p. 146.
53 ibid., 1287 b, Barker, p. 147.
54 *Ethics,* VIII, xiii, 1162 b, Thomson, p. 253.
55 M. Ostwald, *Nomos and the Beginnings of Athenian Democracy* (Oxford, 1969).
56 *Rhetoric,* I, x, 1368 b (translation based on Ingram Bywater's).
57 ibid., xiii, 1373 b (translation by Barker, *Politics,* op. cit., Appendix II, p. 369).
58 W. F. R. Hardie, *Aristotle's Ethical Theory* (Oxford, 1968), p. 205.
59 *Ethics,* V, vii, 1135 a, Thomson, p. 158.

Chapter V

The Pursuit
of the Actual

The study of politics, Aristotle emphasises in the first section of Book IV, must include the actual as much as the ideal. Aristotle is as insistent as Machiavelli or Bacon on the need for the political thinker to take account of the practical realities of political life, distasteful to the strict idealist as they may be. Aristotle does not however take this practical orientation to imply that the ideal norms of human conduct can be neglected as irrelevant. This effort to keep one eye on the ideal norms of politics while not losing touch with current political actualities leads Aristotle to a type of political gradualism: 'The sort of constitutional system which ought to be proposed is one which men can be easily induced, and will be readily able, to graft on to the system they already have. It is as difficult a matter to reform an old constitution as it is to construct a new one; as hard to unlearn a lesson as it was to learn it initially.'[1] The provision of laws for a community depends on the kind of constitution it possesses; hence the need for the correct assessment of the constitutional form of each *polis*. This constitutional form, as Aristotle has already stated in Book III, is conditioned by the distribution of power between the social classes making up a particular *polis*:

A constitution is an arrangement in regard to the offices of the state. By this arrangement the citizen body distributes office, either on the basis of the *power* of those who receive it, or on the basis of some sort of *equality* existing among all who receive it (i.e. the power of the rich *or* the poor, or – if equality be the basis – an equality existing among both rich *and* poor). There must therefore be as many constitutions as there are modes of arranging the distribution of office according to the superiorities and the differences of the parts of the state.[2]

Aristotle refers to the opinion of many in his time who believed that all constitutional classifications could be reduced to a basic division between oligarchy and democracy. Many modern students of Greek politics share this view; thus one of them, Donald Kagan, entitles his general history of Greek political thought *The Great Dialogue*, to indicate his conviction that the whole of Greek political speculation revolves round the oligarchical–democratic antithesis. Aristotle does not however himself accept this. Given his doctrine of the Mean, it is hard to see how he could. Instead he makes clear that his approach will be to present a middle way between extreme perversions, for which he presents musical analogies: 'these perversions will be oligarchical when (like perversions of the Dorian mode) they are more than ordinarily severe and dominant, and democratic when (like perversions of the Phrygian mode) they are soft and relaxed'.[3] Aristotle does not mention the polity here, but it is clear that he has in mind some political combination which will reconcile features of both democracy and oligarchy.

Aristotle concentrates first on democracy and its variants. He distinguishes five types:

(1) Based on strict numerical equality, but necessarily resulting in majority government for the common people.

(2) Based on a property qualification.

(3) Based on confining citizenship to those of 'unimpeachable descent' (i.e. of strict native stock). This was actually the practice in Athens, as we can see from the questions put to candidates for the highest civic offices, as reported in *The Athenian Constitution*:[4]

Who is your father, and to what deme does he belong?
Who is your paternal grandfather?
Who is your mother?
Who is her father, and what is his deme?
Have you an ancestral Apollo and a household Zeus?
Have you a family tomb, and where is it?
Do you treat your parents well?
Do you pay your taxes?
Have you done your military service?

The mention of the law as 'the final sovereign' is intended probably by Aristotle to indicate that nevertheless Athens does not fulfil all the conditions of this type of democracy for, as indicated often elsewhere, Aristotle regards Athenian democracy as subordinating law to the popular will.

(4) A variant of (3), but more liberal in its extension of citizenship.

(5) An extreme and undesirable form, dealt with by Aristotle at

greater length than any of the others and clearly intended to be a description of Athenian conditions. We get the typical anti-Athenian criticisms – that the decrees passed at popular whim supersede the laws, making the *demos* in effect a tyrant, that the gullible mass of the citizens is played upon by demagogues, who flatter the popular assembly by encouraging its belief that everything must be subject to its decision. Aristotle questions whether this type of government should even be called a democracy, because 'everything is managed only by decrees' and 'decrees can never be general rules' giving a stable basis needed by every constitutional structure.[5] Later we shall consider whether Aristotle's criticisms of Athenian democracy are in fact completely substantiated.

Aristotle then turns to make a classification of different types of oligarchy on the same lines:

(1) Based on a property qualification 'high enough to exclude the poor – although they form the majority'[6] but in which presumably all can vote – something like the Solonian constitution.
(2) Based on confining elective rights as well as eligibility for office to a small circle of wealthy property owners.
(3) Based on an hereditary closed corporation.
(4) 'A junto or dynasty' (as Barker happily translates)[7] in which a family group governs as a tyranny without paying any attention to law.

Aristotle's native concern with stubborn pragmatic facts leads him to qualify even these careful classifications with the remark that in practice democratic and oligarchic forms could merge into each other by various permutations, particularly in the fluid situation after a revolution.

Aristotle has up to now been distinguishing between oligarchy and democracy on the basis of their *political structure*; he now turns to make distinctions on the basis of their *social make-up*.

He argues that the first form of democracy will tend to be law-abiding because the agricultural class holds supremacy. This class will be 'able to live by their work, but unable to enjoy any leisure'[8] and hence will meet in assembly only infrequently. Aristotle obviously believes that the less meetings of the citizen body in full assembly the better. Aristotle favours this system of *de facto* curtailing of popular debate to an outright exclusion of the masses from citizenship, as 'the want of sufficient means prevents the enjoyment of leisure'[9] '(which is needed for political activity)' as Barker adds. The emphasis on leisure in this and later sections of Book IV is noteworthy. Leisure is thought of as not merely free time, but as the opportunity for creatively constructive activity, which is summed up in the life of the *polis*. Leisure again plays the key role in the assessment of the social character of the second form of democracy, in which all who possess irreproachable descent are legally allowed to share, but only share in practice when they are able to find the necessary leisure. In the third and fourth forms of democracy financial means rather than leisure is the determining factor. The final form, that of the radical Athenian democracy, is associated by Aristotle with the extension of leisure to engage in politics to all citizens as a result of public subsidisation of the poor by the *polis*. Aristotle argues that the paid proletariat which was the feature of this sort of democracy would have in effect more leisure than any other social section: 'They are not hindered in any way by the duty of attending to private affairs; the well-to-do are, with the result that they often absent themselves from the assembly and the courts. Under these conditions the mass of the poor become the sovereign power in the constitution instead of the laws.'[10] Aristotle does not really make clear why mass popular government should be incompatible with rule in accordance with law. Presumably he feels that such popular government will carry with it a danger of rule by decree instead of stable laws.

Aristotle then deals with the various types of oligarchy, again from a social point of view. The first is a system in which most citizens are moderately well-off property owners. 'Since the generality [of citizens] are thus included in the enjoyment of constitutional rights, it follows that sovereignty – will be rested in the law, and not in persons.'[11] It is hard to see why majority rule in this case should be compatible with the rule of law, though not in the case of democracy.

The second form of oligarchy is more restrictive; property holders are fewer but individually more wealthy and, while preserving outward subordination to the law, they manage to manipulate it to their own advantage. The other two forms of oligarchy are discussed in a similar manner to their treatment earlier in the book.

Before Aristotle proceeds to outline his policy, the mean between oligarchy and democracy, he deals briefly with aristocracy. For him the only true aristocracy is that where 'the good man and the good citizen are absolutely identical'[12] – in other words, the ideal state. He admits however that some forms of government may be described as aristocratic in a relative sense; these are where moral worth as well as wealth is a criterion of eligibility for political office.

Polity is defined by Aristotle as 'a mixture' of oligarchy and

89

democracy 'but in common usage the name is confined to those mixtures which incline to democracy'.[13] This is because, Aristotle tells us a little later, the elements fused in a polity are economically determined – this regime is a combination of the rich and poor. Aristocracy, on the other hand, includes a criterion of merit in addition to the two other elements. The polity manages to bridge the gap between the rich and poor social and political extremes by introducing as a decisive and determining factor, in true Aristotelean fashion, a third social element which will act as a moderating mean between the two others. This is the middle class, whose preponderance, Aristotle a little later declares, will provide the best practicable constitution short of the ideal.

Aristotle argues that this middle class will avoid the ethical vices which plague the other two classes; they will not be domineering like the rich, nor flattering and servile like the poor. Among the middle class a spirit of equality will prevail and this will promote the friendship which is the cementing band of every *polis*. Wherever such a middle class is either more powerful than the other two combined or at least able to act as the deciding factor in the rivalry between rich and poor, Aristotle holds that there will be stable government. Aristotle believes that larger states are more likely to be stable than smaller ones because they do possess this steadying middle-class factor. He goes as far as to attribute greater staying power to democratic as compared with oligarchical regimes because the middle class in democracies 'is more numerous, and is allowed a large share in the government, than it is in oligarchies'.[14] In fact, it is probably correct to say that the polity may be described as a 'limited democracy'.

Aristotle is not unaware of the lack of good auspices for securing this type of middle-class control in most Greek states of his time. Thucydides had already pointed out that the conditions of the Peloponnesian War had tended to crush the middle classes between the upper oligarchic and nether democratic millstones and Aristotle follows up by pointing out that this is facilitated by the fact that 'the middle class is in most states generally small; and the result is that as soon as one or other of the two main classes – the owners of property and the masses – gains the advantage it oversteps the mean, and drawing the constitution in its own direction it institutes, as the case may be, either a democracy or an oligarchy'.[15] This unreadiness to compromise is reflected in the practice of the two great oligarchic and democratic archetypes, Sparta and Athens respectively, who insist on enforcing their own preferred regime on cities within their political orbit.

We should perhaps beware of supposing that Aristotle's middle class has much resemblance to the modern bourgeoisie. We have already seen that Aristotle disliked the financial and commercial basis which tends to be the hallmark of the modern middle class and which in his own time would be more obviously identified with oligarchy. It is equally clear that he does not have in mind anything like the modern petit bourgeois social stratum – shopkeeper, tradesman, etc. These of course existed in Greek cities like Athens but were regarded by Aristotle as not possessing the modicum of leisure necessary for consciously intelligent exercise of citizenship. It seems that the social type which Aristotle envisages as the pillar of his polity is the averagely well-off country gentleman of independent means, the sort of citizen who would be able to fit himself out for military service in the infantry at his own expense – in other words, the *hoplite* as known to Greek history. This class was in social eclipse by Aristotle's time; but he rests on it his hopes for a revival of Greek greatness.

The concept of a middle, moderate form of government was not original to Aristotle. The principle that the good life for man lay in the avoidance of excess and the respect of limits had been a recurrent theme of Greek literature and philosophy. Every worshipper at Delphi, the most sacred of Greek temples, would see the motto inscribed there: 'Take the middle course.' We have already seen (in Chapter I) how the theme of a central principle of moderation and harmony through compromise had had a long history in Athens from the period of Solon onwards, and how it had found supreme imaginative expression in the work of Aeschylus. In the closing stages of the Peloponnesian War it again formed the rallying cry for the party of 'moderates' led by Theramenes, who were disillusioned by the direction taken by the democracy and who managed in 411 to manipulate a change of constitution in a restrictive sense. The main feature of the new constitution was a limitation of citizen rights to the 5,000 or so members of the *hoplite* class. This constitution is mentioned with approval by Thucydides as the best Athens ever had; it is also mentioned with approval by Aristotle or whoever wrote *The Athenian Constitution*: 'Under this new regime Athens would seem to have been well governed; it was a time of war, and the constitution was on a military footing',[16] though the last phrase may imply that the author thought the virtues of the regime to be particularly, perhaps exclusively, suited to wartime conditions. Theramenes, the main architect of this constitution, may be referred to in the *Politics* itself: 'One man, and one only, of all who have hitherto been in a position of ascendancy, has allowed himself to be persuaded to agree to the setting up of such a type'[17] though an alternative interpretation of this passage would regard it as referring to Antipater, who governed Greece on behalf of Alexander during the latter's absence in Asia, and who may well have been interested in the notion of a 'polity' as recommended by Aristotle.[18] He did in fact impose such a regime on Athens after the death of Aristotle. The regime of Theramenes, despite Thucydides's praise, lasted only a few months; in 410 the revived Athenian navy won a victory over Sparta at Cyzicus and was able to make its weight felt in internal politics by insisting on the revival of the democracy. Theramenes was put to death in 403 by the oligarchic regime of the Thirty Tyrants which, under Plato's uncle, Critias, seized power for a while after the ending of the war by the defeat of Athens. Theramenes's defence at his trial, as reported by Xenophon, bears a striking resemblance to Solon's defence of himself in his poems. He argued that he had pleased neither the democrats nor the oligarchs because of his central policy, and there is no doubt that he and Solon were the practical archetypes of the 'polity' as Aristotle envisaged it.

Another influence was undoubtedly Plato in the *Laws*, with its elaborate construction of a society in which extremes of wealth and poverty will be avoided, and of constitutional structure which will combine the best elements of monarchy and democracy. Aristotle himself describes Plato's system as a 'polity' in *Politics*, Book II: 'The whole system [i.e. described in the *Laws*] tends to be one neither of democracy nor of oligarchy, but rather an intermediate form, of the sort which is usually called "polity"; the citizens, for example, are drawn only from those who bear arms',[19] though Aristotle criticises Plato as not really including a monarchical element, as promised, but 'only the elements of oligarchy and democracy, with a particular inclination towards oligarchy'.[20] Aristotle's whole tone in this passage seems to indicate greater reserve towards the idea of the polity than he shows in his own presentation of the concept in Book IV:

> If Plato's view in constructing this constitution is that it represents the form which is most readily attainable by most states, he may very well be right; but if he regards it as the form which comes next in merit to his first, or ideal, form of constitution, he is mistaken; one might commend more highly the constitution of Sparta, or some other form of a more aristocratic character.[21]

Aristotle's polity does in fact differ markedly from Plato's by the fact that it is not a 'mixed constitution' in the sense that Plato's regime is; nor is it a mixed constitution in the sense of being a balanced mixture of constitutional features in the style of later ancient writers such as Polybius and Cicero who saw the Roman Republican Constitution as incarnating their ideal. Still less does Aristotle's polity rest on any separation of powers, deliberative, executive and judicial, as with Locke or Montesquieu. Aristotle's uniqueness in this respect lies in his advocacy of the effective limitation of citizenship to the middle class of *hoplite* citizens, and one may guess that the advocation of such a system for Athens was one of the principal practical objectives behind the composition of the *Politics*. This type of constitution might also be the closest practically realisable approximation to the ethical stance of the man of *phronesis* described in the *Ethics*. Aristotle's admiration for the tradition of Solon and Theramenes indicates his conviction that full-scale popular democracy had been a false step for Athens.

An attempt to implement something like Aristotle's polity was in fact made at Athens after Antipater abolished the full democracy, instituted a property qualification for citizenship and suspended subsidies for the poor. Again the principle of return to the Solonian constitution was the slogan.[22] A pupil of the Aristotelean school, Demetrius of Phalerum, was set up by Antipater as virtual dictator, though with no constitutional position. Demetrius balanced the budget with a surplus, conducted the first census in Greek history which revealed a sizeable population for Athens of towards 250,000 and set up new magistrates to enforce new laws against extravagance in grave monuments, banquets and women's dress. He also erected 360 statues of himself throughout the city. Demetrius's power as boss of Athens rested on the presence of a Macedonian garrison in Athens's port of the Piraeus and when this garrison went Demetrius went too. His regime had obviously been so unpopular that the democracy, which now again returned to power, excluded all members of the Aristotelean school of philosophy from the city for a time as being tarred with the same brush. The social flavour of the time is expressed vividly in Menander's comic plays (Menander was a friend of Demetrius) and the *Characters* of Theophrastus (Demetrius's tutor and successor of Aristotle as head of the Lyceum). They make excellent humorous and satirical reading, but it is doubtful whether the conditions they depict were entirely what Aristotle had in mind when elaborating the idea of the polity.

The remainder of Book IV is concerned with what we may describe as various means of gerrymandering in favour of one or other of the types of constitution. Aristotle's advice to both oligarchical and democratic forms of regime is to temper their characteristic features with minor features drawn from their opposite number. It is the same advice which he will give when dealing in Book V with ways of preventing revolution.

We may now turn to Book VI, which is in the nature of an appendix to Book IV. He is again on the topic of the best way of constructing constitutions, but this time with the accent of emphasis (at least in intention) on the *ethos* behind each type of regime. In practice however he largely deserts this theme in favour of more specific constitutional recommendations. At the beginning of his discussion of the construction of a democratic regime Aristotle inserts an interesting short analysis of the democratic way of life, which he defines as centring on the concept of liberty. This concept branches out into two main forms:

(1) 'The interchange of ruling and being ruled',[23] on a basis of numerical equality. Aristotle has previously defined this rotation of office sharing as being an essential part of citizenship in any *polis*, though he qualifies this by saying 'the citizen of our definition is particularly and especially the citizen of a democracy'.[24] Now he explicitly identifies this participation with a democratic political form.

(2) 'Living as you like.' Aristotle regards this as having what amounts to an anti-political ideal as its goal – 'freedom from any interference of government, and, failing that, such freedom as comes from the interchange of ruling and being ruled'.[25] Aristotle is being somewhat disingenuous in bracketing these not necessarily connected concepts. There is certainly no real ground for supposing that Athenian democracy ever entertained as its ideal the sort of individualistic anarchism which the first part of the sentence implies. We may suspect that Aristotle is trying to give substance to his anti-democratic campaign by implying that democracy somehow means the denial of authority to the *polis* itself in the manner of some of the extreme Sophists and Cynics like Diogenes.

The same dislike of the democracy of his own time is visible in Aristotle's discussion of the four varieties of democracy, which repeats his preference for the agricultural population, declared in Book IV to be the best material for a polity. In this type of democracy 'all the citizens will enjoy the three rights of electing the magistrates, calling them to account, and sitting in the law courts; on the other hand the most important offices will be filled by election, and confined to those who can satisfy a property qualification.'[26] The Solonian type of democracy at Athens (or at least what Aristotle

thought it had been) is clearly in mind. By contrast the urban populace which by now formed the effective basis of Athenian democracy
receives scathing mention:

> They lead a poor sort of life and none of the occupations followed
> by a populace which consists of mechanics, shopkeepers and
> day-labourers, leaves any room for excellence. Revolving around
> the market-place and the city centre, people of this class generally
> find it easy to attend the sessions of the popular assembly – unlike
> the farmers who, scattered through the country-side, neither meet
> so often nor feel so much the need for society of this sort.[27]

The only way Aristotle can see of saving the situation from government by this rabble is by insisting that meetings of the assembly cannot
be held without the participation of the agricultural population.
Aristotle feels that democracy, by casting the net of popular participation too widely, will in the end be the architect of its own ruin,
but he admits that it will be hard to counteract the majority support
which this type of go-as-you please government enjoys. 'Most men
find more pleasure in living without any discipline than they find in
a life of temperance.'[28]

Aristotle diagnoses democracy's chief weakness as its dependence
on a poor and therefore irresponsible proletariat. In order to counteract
this weakness, he offers the enlightened advice that the solution is
to aim at making the poor moderately well-off property owners and
so end their dependence on state doles. Surplus revenues should not
be spent on 'bread and circuses' for the masses, but to establish
a permanent fund for purchase of individual plots of land for them,
or to set them up in commerce or agriculture.

Was Aristotle correct in his criticism of democracy? Modern
historical scholarship suggests that he has omitted either from mention
or from any real consideration some important aspects of constitutional life in fourth-century Athens. All the omitted facts are concerned with limitation in effect of the over-riding powers of the mass
assembly, powers which Aristotle asserts throughout the *Politics* to
be unlimited. We may list these important factors which Aristotle
has omitted from consideration:

(1) He hardly mentions the function of the Council, through which
all matters whatsoever which were to be presented to the
Assembly had to be processed. The Council admittedly was
elected from the Assembly in a rotatory fashion and was ultimately responsible to the Assembly. But this *probouleutic*

(preliminary) supervisory power of the Council did in fact place a brake on irresponsible legislation arising from a stampede of mass voting in the Assembly and hence takes some of the point out of Aristotle's criticism of democracy's government by decree instead of due process of law.

(2) The fifth-century democracy had allowed two constitutional channels by which even Assembly decrees might be challenged if anyone thought they were violating the fundamental laws of the city. These were the so-called *graphe paranomon* (appeal against a given law), which gave any person whatever the right to challenge in writing the legality of any decree. The action was brought against the author of the unlawful motion and even sometimes against the president of the Assembly in which it had been voted. The accuser had to support his action by oath and this had the effect of automatically suspending the controversial enactment until its validity had been decided. The decision lay in the hands of a tribunal, composed of at least 1,000 jurors and sometimes of 6,000. If illegality of a law, either in form or substance, was decided, those responsible for introducing the law were heavily fined, sometimes even put to death. After three condemnations on the score of illegality a citizen forfeited the right to make any proposal in the Assembly.

The other constitutional channel for checking illegalities was the *eisangalion,* a kind of impeachment or trial for conduct amounting to treason against the city. The prosecution of Socrates, for example, came under this heading. This was directed rather against individuals than measures and was often reduced in its significance by being used too often and for too petty purposes, e.g. one citizen was prosecuted under this law of treason for persuading a woman to be unfaithful to her husband; another for hiring out some flute players at more than a legally recognised rate. But despite these extravagances the *eisangelion* could obviously provide another check on subversion of the constitution by hasty demagogic measures.

In the fourth century a further system of check was added by the introduction of officials known as *nomothetai.* These were chosen from the Assembly of citizens to the number of 501 or 1,001, and the Assembly handed over to them all its own powers of legal decision. Each year the Assembly voted on all sections of the laws, to ascertain whether revision should be undertaken. If this was felt to be necessary, the commission of *nomothetai* was empowered to take final decisions on the matter. The proceedings before this commission took the form of a trial, in which the advocates of change appeared as plaintiffs against the existing law, defended by speakers chosen by the Assembly. The decision of the *nomothetai* did not need to be ratified by the full Assembly, but was accepted as final. Aristotle does not even mention the existence of the *nomothetai* anywhere in his work.

(3) It is doubtful whether Athens or any other Greek democracy was of quite the 'go-as-you please' type outlined by Aristotle. Certainly the citizens in Athens must have enjoyed considerably more private freedom than in a rigid regime such as Sparta, but it is equally clear that freedom, even of thought, had its definite bounds. Censorship of opinions on morals and religion was certainly more stringent than in a modern democracy; the condemnation of Socrates is an example of this. Perhaps an even more striking case is that of the earlier philosopher Anaxagoras, who was condemned in the mid-fifth century for asserting that the sun was not a god but a large stone about as big as the Peloponnese. Clearly, for better or worse, the democratic regime was not so unrestrictedly liberal as Aristotle would have his hearers and readers believe.

We have previously mentioned grounds for suspecting that Aristotle's omissions are for very definite reasons. It is hard to accept that he was in complete ignorance of the important constitutional features just mentioned and we are therefore forced to the conclusion that he refrained from mentioning them of set purpose. To have referred to these institutions would certainly have weakened his main case of the legal arbitrariness of democracy and the need to change it for a system limited in franchise such as the polity, in which he felt that his ethically superior man would have more opportunity to mould political life according to his own insight. In order to serve this main objective, Aristotle was ready to modify actually existing facts in such a way as to present, if not actually a caricature, at any rate an incomplete picture of the democratic type of constitution as exemplified at Athens.

The remainder of Book VI is concerned with the construction of oligarchical regimes. The first type of oligarchy is identical with Aristotle's polity previously described. Other types of oligarchy are differentiated by respective narrowing of the property qualification for citizenship, culminating in the 'dynasty', or rule by a small family group. Aristotle picks out military force and its distribution as the key to the prospects for survival of oligarchies. He singles out the light-armed infantry and the navy as the key to control of the *polis* in contemporary conditions. In this he may well have been right, as the history of Athens had shown. Aristotle is very definite that an oligarchy must not allow the light-armed infantry to be manned 'exclusively from the masses'.[29] His solution is: 'A distinction of age-groups should be made; and while they are in the lower age-group, the sons of oligarchs should also be instructed in light-infantry drill and weapons.'[30] This book ends with a listing of the various offices which are a necessary feature of the organisation of all states. Aristotle mentions in passing the office of general (*strategos*)[31] so important in democratic Athens, which could be held for years in succession by popular election by candidates who retained the people's confidence, such as Pericles. Aristotle neglects to point out the importance of this office in providing a continuity which he has accused democratic regimes of lacking. This is yet another illustration of Aristotle's habit of only slight mention or no mention at all of constitutional features which hardly fitted in with his general political thesis. The same would apply to his reference a few lines later[32] to the Council; no one would guess from this brief reference that the Council in democratic Athens occupied the focal position which it actually did.

We now turn back to Book V, which deals with the reasons for the disruption of the various types of *polis* and the means Aristotle recommends for preventing this fate in each case. The modern word 'revolution' is perhaps too sweeping to be a really correct translation of Aristotle's word *stasis*, which has more of the connotation of faction or discord between groups which may, though not always, resort to violence to achieve changes in the structure of the *polis* for their own benefit. That gradualism in the process is not ruled out is shown by Aristotle's remark on change in aristocracies:

A general observation which has already been made in regard to all types of constitutions – that even trifles may be the cause of revolutions – is particularly true of aristocracies. They are especially apt to change imperceptibly, through being undermined little by little. Once they have abandoned one of the elements of the constitution, they find it easier afterwards to alter some other feature of a little greater importance; and they end eventually by altering the whole system of the state.[33]

This could be a summary of the history of modern England.

The relativism of Aristotle's approach to political change has often been pointed out. It clearly owes much to the influence of contemporary medical teaching in its attempts to diagnose the diseases which beset current political forms and the prescriptions given to cure them. Aristotle's connection with the Hippocratic medical tradition, which may even antedate his period at the Academy, has already been mentioned, but the Hippocratic school in its turn had strong affinities with the current of Sophistic teaching which swept the Greek world in the fifth century. Both movements had in common the programme of abandoning any search for abstract generalised explanations of phenomena in the manner of the pre-Socratic natural philosophers and instead concentrating on the observable behaviour of phenomena and predictions based on this empirical knowledge. The point is brought out by the treatise *On Ancient Medicine* (a surviving remnant of the Hippocratic corpus) which argues that in matters of health nothing is absolutely good or absolutely bad; the value of foods, medicines and other means to health is conditioned by the individual state of their respective users. A meal of meat may be good for a man in the best of health; it may be most inappropriate and harmful for one who is ill. The same relativism is found in the surviving fragments of Sophistic writings from such exponents as Protagoras and Gorgias. Protagoras's famous dictum 'Man is the measure of all things', is probably to be understood as implying that knowledge depends, not on absolute norms, but on situational requirements which confront Man both as individual and species. Man's relationship to the potential objects of his knowledge is the deciding and conditioning factor in creating such knowledge and, equally important, of using it to obtain greater control for Man of his environment. The *Dissoi Logoi*, a collection of specimen logical arguments written at the end of the fifth century, argues that there are always two sides to every question – there is no absolutely correct truth: "Sickness is bad for the sick, good for the physician. Death is bad for the dying, good for the undertakers and tomb makers. Victory is good for the victors, bad for the defeated.'

Gorgias, the other leading Sophist of the later fifth century, argued that virtue was a matter of doing the appropriate thing at the right time;[34] here too there is a rejection of an absolute ethical standard in favour of a type of situational ethical judgement varying according to person and circumstances.

Although Aristotle rejects relativism in ethics and decries the Sophists as political guides in the last pages of the *Ethics*, it is hard not to see his technique in Book V of the *Politics* as an application of their methods. Judgement, assessment and advice on each of the types of regime considered is given in situational terms. Aristotle places himself in turn in the shoes of each of the types of government he is discussing and treats them in terms of their own respective characteristics and objectives. It seems a far cry from the ideal *polis* or even from the virtue of *phronesis*, though there are occasional reversions to absolute norms, as at the end of the section of advice to tyrants, when Aristotle remarks that, if his recommendations are carried out, and the tyrant rules in a temperate fashion, not only will 'his rule be more lasting', but he himself 'will attain a habit of character, if not wholly disposed to goodness, at any rate half-good and half-bad, but at any rate not wholly bad'.[35]

Aristotle's tendency throughout his discussion of revolutionary change is to ascribe the causes of upheaval in the *polis* to personal resentment, unsatisfied ambition and the like. At first sight this may strike the modern reader as rather naive and superficial; in such matters we are all Marxists now. Aristotle is not however putting forward a 'Cleopatra's nose' theory of politics and history; his assertion of the paramount role of personal discontent in *breaking up* a state is a corollary of his belief that the primary motive force in *building up* a state is personal friendship, leading to a collaboration for communal objectives which is stronger than a merely legal relationship;[36] justice itself in a truly political sense depends on a personal inter-relationship between equals, in which all will participate in rotation in the business of government.[37] When such a personal bond is lacking, the *polis* is ripe for dissolution. If Aristotle does not emphasise economic factors in his analysis, it is because he feels that they too are grounded in morals, as the economic life of a political association is grounded on a sense of *koinonia*, a communal solidarity springing from an affective friendship towards one's fellow-citizens.[38]

Aristotle's discussion of suggested means by which each regime known to the Greek world might preserve its stability has often been compared to Machiavelli's approach to politics; presumably the allegedly cynical character of both approaches is the reason for such a comparison. Both are in fact less cynical than they appear to be, for both are basically arguing for the creation of a public spirit of mutual trust among citizens which will demonstrate itself in loyalty towards their rulers. The advice given by both to tyrants is very much of an 'interim ethic' which it is hoped, will eventually lead to a more permanent law-based regime. Aristotle certainly gives totally 'realistic' advice to tyrants who are resolved to preserve their government by force and fraud, just as Machiavelli does so in *The Prince*. But it is obvious in both cases that the author's own preference is in the direction of a more moderate way of government by the tyrant. Aristotle in fact urges his hypothetical tyrant to behave as if he were not a lawless despot – to act as if he were a king exercising authority according to the law. He must appear 'as more of a steward than a tyrant'.[39]

The distinction between the two types of tyrant seems to correspond to an historical distinction which is observable between an earlier type of tyranny such as that of Pisistratus and his family at Athens and a later type, more contemporary with Aristotle, exemplified by the tyrants of Syracuse. The former type did in fact rule ostensibly according to forms of law. Pisistratus, like Augustus in Rome and the Medici in Machiavelli's Florence, allowed the traditional forms of civic government to continue and the offices of state to be held in theory by others, while keeping the real strings of power in his own hands. This earlier type of Greek tyranny (seventh and sixth centuries BC) seems in many cities to have acted as a factor to break the hold of the aristocracies and hence served as the advance guard for the subsequent advent of democracy. These older tyrannies undoubtedly enjoyed much popular support. The revolt which overthrew the Athenian tyranny in 510 BC was originally oligarchical and was carried out initially as a *coup* which did not have the support of the people. This only came later when the revolution broadened under Cleisthenes into a more democratic movement. There is also a theory (put forward by P. N. Ure in *The Origins of Tyranny*) that this older type of tyranny was connected with the beginnings of the Greek economic revolution and was the political expression of the capitalist expansion of the time.

The less favoured type of tyranny seems to correspond with repressive regimes such as that of the Thirty Tyrants at Athens at the end of the fifth century and, in Aristotle's own time, the appearance of the Syracusan tyrants and rulers on the Greek mainland such as Jason of Pherae, in Thesaly. The behaviour of such men seems in fact to have closely corresponded with Aristotle's description and was also reprobated by Plato in the *Republic*. One can see why Aristotle should have given a qualified approval to the older type. In this matter, as in so many others, Aristotle regards his own age as one of political and social deterioration.

Aristotle finishes Book V with some critical notes on Plato's philosophy of constitutional change as set forth in the *Republic*. Aristotle rightly enough points to the anomaly that Plato admits the possibility of deterioration for his ideal *polis*. He takes Plato's enigmatic explanation of the failure of the Guardians to breed in the correct eugenic way because of their failure to observe the mystic number as inadequate; he thinks Plato really means that 'the reproduction of the species sometimes issues in men of poor quality, who are beyond the reach of education'.[40] Aristotle admits there may be something in this, but cannot understand why this cause should be peculiar to the ideal city. Here, as elsewhere in his criticism of Plato, he does not examine the possibility (hinted at by Plato himself) that the description may be purely symbolical, if not ironical, and may not be intended as a serious historical analysis. Aristotle does however treat it seriously, as he does Plato's scheme of decline of one type of regime into another – ideal city into timocracy, into oligarchy, into democracy, into tyranny. Aristotle points out that this scheme can be disproved by historical instances where the development does not take place in this order. It is doubtful however whether Plato meant his scheme to be treated chronologically; its arrangement is rather for logical convenience and is in any case meant to be taken in conjunction with his parallel discussion of the decline of the individual human personality after an abandonment of government of the soul by reason. Aristotle's literalism is responsible for his objection:

> When it comes to tyrannies Plato stops; he never explains whether they do, or do not, change, nor, if they do, why they do so, or into what constitution they change. The reason of this omission is that any explanation would have been difficult. The matter cannot be settled along the lines of his argument; for on those lines a tyranny would have to change back into the first and ideal constitution, in order to maintain continuity in the revolving cycle of change'.[41]

In any case, Aristotle's criticism of Plato in this section of the *Politics* illustrates the abiding legacy of Plato to Aristotle, even in the latter's more empirical moods. The intellectual relationship of the two philosophers leads naturally to the problem of Aristotle's own approach to the question of the 'ideal' *polis*, at first sight so out of step with the general tone of his political thought.

Notes Chapter V

1   *Politics*, IV, i, 1289 a, Barker, p. 156.
2   ibid., 1290 a, Barker, p. 161.
3   ibid., Barker, p. 162.
4   II, 55 (translation by J. Warrington, in Everyman Library edition of the *Politics* and *The Athenian Constitution*, London, 1959, p. 295).
5   *Politics*, IV, iv, 1292 a, Barker, p. 169.
6   ibid.
7   ibid., IV, v, 1292 b, Barker, p. 170.
8   IV, vi, 1292 b, Barker, p. 171.
9   ibid.
10 ibid., 1293 a, Barker, pp. 171–2.
11 ibid., 1293 a, Barker, p. 172.

12 IV, vii, 1293 b, Barker, p. 173.
13 IV, viii, 1293 b, Barker, p. 175.
14 IV, xi, 1296 a, Barker, p. 182.
15 ibid., Barker, p. 185.
16 Translation by Warrington, op. cit., p. 276.
17 *Politics*, IV, xi, 1296 a, Barker, p. 183.
18 P. Andrews, 'Aristotle, *Politics*, IV, xi, 1926 a, 38–40', *Classical Review* (1952), pp. 141–4, claims the 'one man' to be Hermias of Atarneus.
19 *Politics*, II, vi, 1265 b, Barker, p. 60.
20 ibid., 1266 a, Barker, p. 61.
21 II, vi, 1265 b, Barker, p. 60. On variations of outlook towards Sparta by Aristotle in the *Politics*, see R. A. De Laix, 'Aristotle's conception of the Spartan Constitution', *Journal of the History of Philosophy*, XI (1973), pp. 21–30.
22 See P. McKendrick, *The Athenian Aristocracy, 399–31* BC (Cambridge, Mass., 1969).
23 *Politics*, VI, ii, 1317 b, Barker, p. 258.
24 III, i, 1275 b, Barker, pp. 94–5.
25 VI, ii, 1317 b, Barker, p. 258.
26 VI, iv, 1318 b, Barker, p. 264.
27 ibid., 1319 a, Barker, p. 265.
28 ibid., 1319 b, Barker, p. 267.
29 VI, vii, 1321 a, Barker, p. 272.
30 ibid.
31 VI, viii, 1322 a, Barker, p. 276.
32 ibid., 1322 b, Barker, p. 276.
33 V, vii, 1307 a–b, Barker, p. 223.
34 A concept summed up in the word *kairos*.
35 *Politics*, V, xi, 1315 a, Barker, p. 250.
36 For Aristotle's argument, see *Ethics*, V and VIII.
37 F. Rosen, 'The political context of Aristotle's categories of justice', *Phronesis*, XX (1975), pp. 228–40, points out the political importance of 'reciprocity' for Aristotle's theory of tolerable government, and underlines the tension between it and Aristotle's other theory of specialisation by the ethical expert.
38 See M. I. Finley, 'Aristotle and economic analysis', in M. I. Finley (ed.), *Studies in Ancient Society* (London, 1974), pp. 26–52.
39 *Politics*, V, xi, 1314 b, Barker, p. 247.
40 V, xii, 1316 a, Barker, p. 251.
41 ibid., Barker, pp. 251–2.

Chapter VI

The Pursuit
of the Ideal

Book II of the *Politics* is an examination, in historical perspective, of previous attempts to delineate the nature of the *polis* by studying it as an ideal.

Much of the book is occupied with criticism of Plato's *Republic* and *Laws*. At the outset we are struck by a puzzling feature of Aristotle's approach to Plato's views, that is, his arbitrarily selective treatment of Plato's argument. Aristotle concentrates entirely on Plato's suggestions for communism of property and wives, matters which seem to be secondary elements of Plato's general argument. Nothing is said of the place of justice in politics, the necessity of philosophy for correct statesmanship, the education of the philosopher-rulers, the theory of Forms, all much more important aspects of Plato's outlook. One can hardly suppose, as Gilbert Ryle does in his *Plato's Progress*,[1] that Aristotle was ignorant of the parts of the *Republic* in which these matters are discussed. In fact Aristotle does in one place refer to these other sections, but only to discuss them in scathing fashion as irrelevant: 'Plato has filled up the dialogue with digressions extraneous to the main theme, and with a discussion of the proper nature of the education of his guardians'.[2] In order to understand what Aristotle means by 'the main theme', from which he thinks Plato has rambled, one has to remember Aristotle's habit of assessing the philosophies of previous thinkers according to the classifications he has in fact invented for his own. Thus Plato had known nothing of a distinction between theoretical and practical sciences; Aristotle however, as we have seen, sharply differentiated them, and from this point of view he could logically assume that Plato was in fact confusing the two fields. In his *Metaphysics* Aristotle does in fact pay considerable attention to the theory of Forms as expounded in the *Republic*; but from the point of view of the *Politics* this is not relevant because it is not really 'political'. It is beside the point here to inquire whether this method of treatment really does justice to Plato's thought; nor can we embark on the wider question of how far an interpreter is justified in imposing his own classifications on a thinker under study instead of observing those employed by the object of study himself. All that we are concerned with here is that an appreciation of Aristotle's procedure in this matter does give a reasonable explanation of what might otherwise seem an impossibly cavalier and perverse method of treating Plato. The same procedure can in fact be seen in Aristotle's treatment of the *Laws*. Here all mention of Plato's extensive remarks on history, philosophy, religion, science, education and even law itself is omitted and once again the question of property and its distribution alone holds the field.[3]

Aristotle's main criticism of Plato, within these limits, is that in an exaggerated zeal for unity with his communities, both in the *Republic* and the *Laws*, Plato had virtually swallowed up the individual in the *polis*. In doing so, Aristotle contended, Plato had not only stunted the individual but had seriously crippled the *polis* itself because the happiness of the community depended on that of its members: 'It is impossible for the whole of a *State* to be happy unless most of its parts, or all, or at any rate some, are happy.'[4] Aristotle's criticisms of Plato may to a modern reader seem somewhat pedantic and niggling in detail; very possibly the same may be true of his remarks on the proposals of other theorists of the ideal *polis*, Phaleas of Chalcedon and Hippodamus of Miletus, whose writings are lost to us and against which the accuracy of Aristotle's account cannot be checked. What seems clear, whatever the rights and wrongs of Aristotle's criticisms of these theorists, is that he felt that they erred in supposing that man's life in political community could be organised according to precise, quasi-mathematical application of doctrinaire principles, like Phaleas's panacea of equal property division or Hippodamus's belief in rigidly rationalist planning, stemming from the assumption that social life could be mapped out like the patterned topography of a town. All these schemes, felt Aristotle, came to grief because of the inescapable relative inexactitude of practical life: ' . . . in matters of political organization, as in the arts generally, it is impossible for every rule to be written down precisely; rules must be expressed in general terms, but actions are concerned with particulars'.[5] Furthermore, such ultra-rationalist systems allow no room for the character and pace of human change. They attempt too much, is the implication of Aristotle's criticism; the order they attempt to impose can only in fact be realised in the world of theoretical science, and this is a realm of thought which does not include politics.

The rest of Book II is a somewhat puzzling examination of

historically actual 'ideal' States (Sparta, Crete, Carthage and Solonic Athens). They appear paradoxically in the present context because each of them embodies a conscious, if ultimately unsuccessful, effort to keep abreast of change by a constitutional balance of powers between the various social classes making up their communities. The details of the various political structures described are of purely historical interest, but in each case it is clear that Aristotle holds that the attempt to reach a harmonious communal order is doomed because of an inbalance which biases the *polis* concerned in an eccentric direction, and sways it away from the desired 'mixed' constitution which would have saved it from decay.

Books VII and VIII of the *Politics* embody (though in unfinished form) Aristotle's own attempt to construct an ideal *polis* in his mind's eye. First, however, he feels that he has to take the essential preliminary question – what is the ideal life for men, both communally and individually? He starts on this inquiry because of a belief that the best way of life and the best political constitution must, in the nature of things, be intimately connected. This problem in its turn suggests a further important query ' . . . whether or not the same way of life is desirable in the case of the community as in that of the individual'.[6]

The first problem, the character of the best life, obviously goes deep into the heart of ethics and our Chapter IV has already tried to examine some themes of Aristotle's approach to this as presented in the *Nicomachean Ethics*. It must be added here that the present discussion in Book VII of the *Politics* stands closer to Aristotle's less well-known and less comprehensive ethical treatise, *Eudemian Ethics*.[7] In the *Eudemian Ethics* Aristotle presents the ideal of the good life as ' . . . a carefully articulated "mixed" life . . . the life of a philosopher fully engaged in social, political, and family activities'.[8] By contrast, the ideal of happiness and goodness set forth in the *Nicomachean Ethics* is, as we have seen, on the whole, one of strictly intellectualist contemplation, and we have noticed in our Chapter IV how this attitude, particularly in *Nicomachean Ethics*, Book X, creates an ambiguity of approach on Aristotle's part to political life and a definite pessimism with regard to its ultimate possibilities, which are rated far below those of speculative philosophical contemplation.

Book VII of the *Politics* modifies, if it does not entirely reverse, this orientation. In this discussion Aristotle tries to combine the claims of the speculative intellect with those of the more active moral virtues by pointing out that right action, for the *polis* as well as the individuals composing it, must depend upon correct intellectual judgement. Human goodness, though needing a certain minimum of external supports, must be primarily assessed in terms of the goodness of the soul, or, as we might put it in modern terms, the character or personality.

Aristotle's conception of the soul is one of the most puzzling ambiguities in his *Corpus* of writings. The *De Anima* (his most elaborate treatise on the nature of the soul) embodies in a nutshell the very different interpretations of the soul's nature and functions which he managed to entertain without any apparent sense of incongruity. For most of the treatise Aristotle appears to regard the soul as the Form which gives meaning and individual personality to the bodily matter making up each human being. There seems to be no hint at this stage of any theory of immortality of the soul in a Platonic or any other sense. But towards the end of *De Anima* (III, v) Aristotle, in discussing the cognitive functions of the soul, begins to talk about 'active and passive' types of intellectual functioning, of which the former type appears to be over and above the rest of the individual human compound, and to be in fact something immortally existing in its own right. 'When mind is set free from its present conditions,' he tells us, 'it appears as just what it is and nothing more; this alone is immortal and eternal (we do not, however, remember its former activity because, while mind in this sense is impassible, mind as passive is destructible), and without it nothing thinks.'[9] This passage would seem to imply a soul-body dualism very reminiscent of Plato's conception of unitary psychic immortality as expressed in a number of his dialogues,[10] complete with the doctrine of reincarnation, expressed in the reference to the soul's 'former activity'. There has been a tremendous amount of controversy through the ages on this baffling aspect of Aristotle's theory of the soul. Many modern interpreters have been understandably anxious to explain it away as a muddled aberration or rhetorical flourish, but it occurs at so crucial a point of the argument of *De Anima* and seems to be expressed so emphatically and carefully by Aristotle that the most obvious interpretation of the passage must be that Aristotle definitely meant to imply that a certain attribute of immortal activity was inherent in the nature of the soul. This would certainly tie up with the injunction in Book X of the *Nicomachean Ethics* which we have met in a previous chapter. We noted there how Aristotle sang the praises of the contemplative intellect and encouraged those who wished to follow its promptings in the daring pursuit of absolute truth. In that passage of the *Nicomachean Ethics*[11] Aristotle links the pursuit of speculative truth with the immortal, 'sovereign and better part of Man'.[12] In the *Metaphysics* too God, the only completely perfect and divine being in the universe, is defined primarily as self-contained and self-subsistent Thought.[13]

This trend of Aristotle's thought, in which pure contemplation appears to be indicated as *the* most characteristic mark of both Divine and human being, sits not altogether easily with the interest shown in the *Eudemian Ethics* and in the last two books of the *Politics* in a more comprehensive and less exclusively intellectualist definition of human goodness and happiness.[14] In fact this fundamental tension in Aristotle's thought on this subject appears to suggest a very significant ambiguity in his view of political life.

Does he leave this ambiguity unresolved?

For the moment, however, we return to the second part of Aristotle's main inquiry – whether happiness for the state is of the same character as individual happiness. Aristotle's discussion of this question is not very clear and is in fact more concerned with the discussion of the best life for the *polis*; Aristotle soon decides that the 'issue of what is good for the individual' falls outside the scope 'of political thought and political speculation'[15] which is the subject under survey at the moment. One may note here that Aristotle appears at this point to be separating in effect politics from ethics, which is a departure from his normal procedure. He is not however in the event able to preserve any such distinction, for the argument resolves itself into discussion of the relative merits of the philosophical and political lives, as led by both individual and state. As Aristotle himself words the problem: 'Which way of life is the more desirable? The way of politics and action? Or the way of detachment from all external things – the way, let us say, of contemplation, which some regard as the only way that is worthy of a philosopher?'[16]

The discussion of the individual–*polis* analogy, which Aristotle, it is probable, borrowed from Plato in the *Republic*, soon becomes a discussion on the tendency of authority to become tyrannical domination. The temptation of all more powerful Greek cities to become chauvinistically imperialistic is at the centre of Aristotle's reasoning here:

> There are some who dislike the exercise of authority over neighbouring states. They regard it as the height of injustice when the authority is despotic; they still regard it as a hindrance to one's well-being, if not as an injustice to others, when the authority is constitutional.[17]

Aristotle's view of the driving force behind the states of his time is jaundiced; personal and public ambition and lust for conquest is singled out by him as the motivation of the average government. If

Aristotle is indeed a political 'naturalist' it is a Nature red in tooth claw which he certainly presents here; his profound pessimism and distrust of politics as actually practised would almost link him with later critics of human authority on religious grounds, such as for example, St Augustine. In advance too he has condemned the whole host of 'realistic' theories of politics associated with such writers as Machiavelli, and has rejected the notion that politics has a right to autonomy from the ethical norms which govern the individual. In the following extract he lines up with Plato's Socrates against the illogical egotism of Callicles or Thrasymachus:

> Conquerors may be in the wrong. There is no profession in which we can find a parallel for statesmanship of this type. Doctors and pilots are never expected to use coercion or cajolery in handling their patients or crews. But when it comes to politics most people appear to believe that mastery is the true statesmanship; and men are not ashamed of behaving to others in ways which they refuse to acknowledge as just, or even expedient, among themselves.[18]

An almost Utopian contrast is pictured a little later:

> It is possible to imagine a solitary State which is happy in itself and in isolation. Assume such a State, living somewhere or other all by itself, and living under a good system of law. It will obviously have a good constitution; but the scheme of its constitution will have no regard to war, or to the conquest of enemies, who, upon our hypothesis, will not exist.[19]

If neighbours do exist, Aristotle admits that some form of military preparedness will have to be kept in being, but he is anxious to argue that military activity is not, as much former Greek practice and theory would have it, the principal end of the activity of the *polis*. The principal end for Aristotle is instead '. . . the enjoyment of partnership in a good life and the felicity thereby attainable'. He has parted company decisively with the cult of competitive individual excellence summed up in previous Greek culture by the concept of *arete*. Aristotle now moves on to a reconsideration of the question which had preoccupied him in Book X of the *Ethics*; which life is preferable, that of contemplation or that of action? In the present passage of the *Politics*[20] Aristotle reaches a harmonious solution by denying that there is any real incompatibility between the two types of life, when each is taken at its best. Only when the active life is based on friendly reciprocal relationship between like-minded individuals (as should be the case in the ideal *polis*) is there no conflict. Once more we see how the theme of friendship and personal harmony enables Aristotle to solve a major dilemma arising from contrasting portions of his theory. Even states and individuals who prefer to live in isolation from others need not be completely without connection with the active life. In a very profound insight Aristotle holds that their very contemplative thought is itself action.[21] Aristotle's conception is here not far away from the mysticism which made Plotinus declare in his *Enneads* that all of nature is in a sense contemplative, or from the Christian monastic ideal in which the enclosed contemplative represents in some degree in his prayers and meditations the lay believer who leads his life in the outside world.

Aristotle's detailed discussion of the ideal state owes something to Hippocratic influences (the optimum size, geographical situation, and so on) but rather more to the Platonic tradition, reinterpreted in characteristically original fashion.

Even though Aristotle is now describing the ideal state, he does not talk, as Plato had done, in terms of education for philosophers. In fact it is here that the man of *phronesis* comes into his own and it is the ideal training for him that Aristotle has in mind. We are back again at the question posed at the end of the *Ethics* – that of constructing a *polis* fit for the man of *phronesis* to live in – and Aristotle now returns to the problem, fortified by his examination of the theoretical and factual bases of the *polis* as it is in actuality. In his ideal system 'all should share alike in a system of government under which they rule and are ruled by turns'.[22] Aristotle admits that there must be a distinction of quality between governors and governed. But instead of, like Plato, making this a matter of lifelong class stratification, he bases it on the distinction between youth and maturity; thus every citizen, once he has attained the correct stage of development, will be able to have his turn at ruling. This is very much in keeping with the emphasis on growth and development in Aristotle's general philosophy.

Aristotle starts the education of his citizens from infancy. Even on child care he takes issue with Plato: 'Plato, in his *Laws*, would like to stop children from straining their lungs and sobbing'[23] but Aristotle is less indulgent towards the infants: 'It [i.e. crying] helps the growth of children; it is, in its way, a sort of physical exercise; and just as holding the breath gives adults strength for exertion so straining the lungs will equally strengthen children.'[24]

For education of older children and youths Aristotle follows what amounts to a variant on what was the already existing Greek educational practice, which divided educational training into reading, writing, physical training and music. Fourth-century Greece was an extremely literate society and Aristotle was taking contemporary conditions for granted by assuming an at any rate average standard of literacy for his ideal citizens. Physical training too is worthwhile for all, but he criticises Sparta for overemphasising the kind of athletic professionalism that is valuable only to the competitive few and can be actually debilitating to those who should be devoting their time to mental activity.

Music is ideal for higher education because it can reproduce in the individual images of states of character in anger, sorrow and calm – which can lead to the development of special sensitivity and the purging (*catharsis*) of unwanted passion through a harmless safety valve. Aristotle's short discussion of *catharsis* here is similar to his more elaborate treatment and his *Poetics* and may be contrasted with Plato's more rigorous insistence in the *Republic* that all poetry should be banished from the ideal *polis* in order that this very emotional identification should not take place. Music for Aristotle includes of course the whole range of drama and poetry which for the Greeks inevitably had a musical background. His conservatism comes out in details like his preference for the lyre, the instrument of the older epic and lyric tradition, as against the flute, which was associated in his time with a more popular and orgiastic type of dancing and drama.

Aristotle's discussion of music, with which the *Politics* as it stands comes to an end, is perhaps an epitome of his outlook throughout, with its corresponding merits and demerits. Profoundly conservative to the point of bias, a bias which often leads him to distort the facts, Aristotle yet manages to preserve a belief in growth and development which made his philosophy a seminal force in societies very different from the Greece of his own time. His criticism of Plato, petty as it often is, was yet useful as a corrective to the more complex older master, at once idealist and sceptic as he was. Aristotle is neither, exclusively; he is a rationalist system builder, but he is never far from the groundwork of empirical observation and it is in this combination that his greatest appeal lies. He stands as the perfect embodiment of his own man of *phronesis*, an all too uncommon actor on any political scene. Aristotle, like Aeschylus, could not save the *polis*. But, also like the old dramatist, he was able to indicate for future and perhaps more lucky societies the qualities of moderation, reciprocity and above all genuine community in the harmonious reconciliation of conflicting opponents, from which alone could be expected political salvation. This was the philosophical complement of the tragic vision and from it alone could flow a satisfying union of contemplation and action.

111

Notes Chapter VI

1 Cambridge, 1966.
2 *Politics*, II, vi, 1264 b, Barker, pp. 56–7.
3 See G. Morrow, 'Aristotle's comments on Plato's *Laws*', in I. Düring and G. E. Owen (eds), *Aristotle and Plato in the Mid-Fourth Century* (Göteborg, 1960), pp. 145–62, which argues that Aristotle's treatment of Plato is not, in most instances, arbitrary.
   On the treatment of Plato's political writings by Aristotle in the *Politics* I have profited from suggestions by Mr D. D. Hall, of the University of Swansea, whose unpublished work on Plato's irony discusses this problem in some detail.
4 Politics, II, v, 1244 b, Barker, p. 54.
5 II, viii, 1269 a, Barker, p. 73.
6 VII, i, 1323 a, Barker, p. 279.
7 See the plausible argument in favour of this in J. M. Cooper, *Reason and Human Good in Aristotle* (Harvard, 1975), p. 142, n. 57.
8 Cooper, op. cit., p. 145.
9 *De Anima* (*On the Soul*), III, v, 430 a (translation by J. A. Smith, in W. D. Ross (ed.), *Oxford Translation of the Works of Aristotle*; reprinted in R. McKeon, *Introduction to Aristotle*, 2nd edn, Chicago, 1973, pp. 230–1.
10 Though in some of them Plato himself seems to be in two minds on the issue (e.g. the *Republic's* vacillations between a tripartite and a unitary soul).
11 *Ethics*, X, vii, 1178 a, Thomson, p. 305.
12 ibid.
13 *Metaphysics*, XII, vii, 1072 b and ix, 1074 b.
14 Or 'flourishing', as Cooper, op. cit., pp. 89–90, attractively suggests as a substitute for the usual rendering of 'happiness' as the translation of Aristotle's *eudaimonia*.
15 *Politics*, VII, ii, 1324 a, Barker, p. 284.
16 ibid.
17 ibid.
18 ibid., 1324 b, Barker, pp. 285–6.
19 ibid., 1325 a, Barker, p. 286.
20 ibid.
21 VII, iii, 1325 a–b, Barker, pp. 287–9.
22 VII, xiv, 1332 b, Barker, p. 315.
23 VII, xvii, 1336a, Barker, p. 329.
24 ibid.

Selected Bibliography

A TRANSLATIONS OF ARISTOTLE'S WORKS

All of Aristotle's *Corpus*, genuine and doubtful, has been translated into English. The best overall series is that published by Oxford University Press between 1908 and 1952 under the title of *The Works of Aristotle translated into English* (12 volumes, under the general editorship of Sir W. D. Ross and J. A. Smith). Of this series the volumes which particularly concern the subject matter of the present book are Vol. IX, 1925 (*The Nicomachean* and *Eudemian Ethics*, translated by W. D. Ross and J. Solomon respectively, and the *Magna Moralia*, translated by St George Stock); Vol. X, 1921 (*The Politics*, translated by B. Jowett (revised for this edition), *The Oeconomica*, translated by E. S. Forster, and *The Constitution of Athens*, translated by Sir F. G. Kenyon); Vol. XII, 1952 (the *Early Fragments* (including the *Protrepticus*) translated by Sir W. D. Ross). T. W. Organ, *An Index to Aristotle in English Translation* (Princeton, NJ, 1949) is a lexicon intended to be used with the Oxford translation. Another complete translation of the *Corpus* is in the Loeb Classical series (Heinemann, London), of which the version of the *Nicomachean Ethics* by A. Rackham (revised edition, 1934) may be particularly singled out as helpful; all the Loeb translations include the Greek text on facing pages. A convenient cheap modern translation of *The Nicomachean Ethics* by J. A. K. Thomson is included in the Penguin Classics series (Harmondsworth, 1955). For the *Politics* may above all be recommended the translation by Sir E. Barker, *The Politics of Aristotle* (Oxford, 1946), with copious notes and a long introduction; the unabridged edition of this book is preferable. Another good recent translation of the *Politics* is by J. Warrington, *Aristotle's Politics and the Athenian Constitution* (Everyman Library: London, Dent, 1959), while Warrington has also produced the most accessible and convenient version of the *Metaphysics* (Everyman Library: London, Dent, 1956). Readable recent versions of the *Poetics* are included in *Classical Literary Criticism*, translated by T. S. Dorsch (Penguin Classics, Harmondsworth, 1965), and in *Ancient Literary Criticism* (M. E. Hubbard's translation), edited by D. A. Russell and M. Winterbottom (Oxford, 1972). R. McKeon's excellent anthology, *Introduction to Aristotle* (2nd edn, Chicago, 1973) contains complete versions of the *Posterior Analytics, Nicomachean Ethics, De Anima (On the Soul)* and the *Poetics*, and lengthy extracts from the *Physics, Metaphysics, Politics, On the Parts of Animals* and the *Rhetoric*, all reprinted from the Oxford translation and with a long and helpful introduction by the editor; anyone wanting an attractive initial confrontation with Aristotle at first hand could do no better than use this book. *The Athenian Constitution* is the subject of two recent annotated versions, those by K. von Fritz and E. Kapp, *Aristotle's Constitution of Athens and Related Texts* (New York, 1950), and by J. M. Moore, *Aristotle and Xenophon on Democracy and Oligarchy* (London, 1975). *The Protrepticus* has been translated by I. Düring, *Aristotle's Protrepticus: An attempt at reconstruction* (Göteborg, 1961).

B   MODERN SECONDARY WORKS ON ARISTOTLE

The best overall and concise account of Aristotle's philosophical system as a whole is in A. Edel, *Aristotle* (New York, 1967), which contains a well-chosen anthology of translated selections from the various branches of Aristotle's writings. All the standard general histories of philosophy contain more or less comprehensive outlines of Aristoteleanism, but a number of modern stimulating detailed accounts exist. Of these may be mentioned J. H. Randall, *Aristotle* (New York, 1960), which is always eminently readable and thought-provoking, but which sometimes distorts Aristotle's thought in the interests of 'modernising' it; H. B. Veatch, *Aristotle: A Contemporary Appreciation* (Bloomington, Indiana, 1974), clear and readable, but also too preoccupied with demonstrating Aristotle's contemporary relevance; S. Clark, *Aristotle's Man* (Oxford, 1974) is another 'committed' study which yet manages to stick more closely to Aristotle's own statements: this is probably the most brilliantly original of recent books on Aristotle. More traditional scholarly introductions, which confine themselves to sound and businesslike interpretations of the texts are D. W. Ross, *Aristotle* (5th edn, London, 1949) – an invaluable but stodgy reference book by a great Aristotelean scholar who was capable of writing better than he does here; D. J. Allan, *The Philosophy of Aristotle* (Oxford, 1952), attractive and readable; G. R. G. Mure, *Aristotle*, (London, 1932), which is sometimes involved and difficult and practically ignores the *Politics*; and G. E. R. Lloyd, *Aristotle: The Growth and Structure of his Thought* (Cambridge, 1968) – reliable and comprehensive. W. Jaeger, *Aristotle: Fundamentals of the History of his Development* (English trans., 2nd edn, Oxford, 1948), was the pioneering classic of modern Aristotelean studies, though few would now accept its conclusions *in toto*; it tries to work out the chronology and sequence of Aristotle's intellectual evolution, which it sees as a progressive emancipation from the influence of Plato. M. A. Grene, *A Portrait of Aristotle* (London, 1963), emphasises the scientific and pragmatic orientation of Aristotle's approach to philosophy, though the author overstates her case. E. Voegelin, *Order and Society, Vol. III: Plato and Aristotle* (Baton Rouge, Louisiana, 1957) is often partisan and speculative, but contains many suggestive insights. A.-H. Chroust, *Aristotle: New light on his life and on some of his lost works* (2 vols, London, 1973), is a collection of essays, old and new, by this erudite and exciting off-beat scholar. A. E. Taylor, *Aristotle* (revised edn, London, 1943) is too inclined to make points against Aristotle in favour of Plato.

The problems of the foundation and character of the Lyceum are discussed magisterially by J. P. Lynch, *Aristotle's School: A study of a Greek educational institution* (Berkeley and Los Angeles, 1972) and, more eccentrically, by F. Grayeff, *Aristotle and his School* (London, 1974).

The only attempt at a full-scale treatment in English of Aristotle's political thought to have been made in the present century is E. Barker, *The Political Thought of Plato and Aristotle* (London, 1906); though this is sound and balanced and still of value, it is inevitably becoming outdated. The *Ethics* has been better served by recent scholars; W. F. R. Hardie, *Aristotle's Ethical Theory* (Oxford, 1968) is an outstanding study, while C. J. Rowe, *The Eudemian and Nicomachean Ethics: A study in the development of Aristotle's Thought* (Cambridge, 1971), and J. D. Moran, *Moral Knowledge and its Methodology in Aristotle* (Oxford 1968) analyse Aristotle's ethical treatises from different standpoints. M. Hamburger, *Morals and Law: The*

Growth of Aristotle's Legal Theory (New Haven, 1951), is an original survey of its topic, though he departs from the majority scholarly opinion by accepting the authenticity of the *Magna Moralia*. J. L. Stocks, *Aristoteleanism* (London and New York, 1925) contains a short but useful survey of the subsequent development of Aristotelean philosophy in later times.

C BACKGROUND BOOKS ON GREEK HISTORY AND THOUGHT

Short and well-written books on the general historical and cultural background include H. D. F. Kitto, *The Greeks* (Harmondsworth, Penguin, 1951); W. G. Forrest, *The Emergence of Greek Democracy* (London, 1966); and (most comprehensive), A. Andrews, *Greek Society* (Harmondsworth, Penguin, 1971). An attractively written and illustrated larger book is A. Levesque, *The Greek Adventure* (London, 1968). A. H. M. Jones, *Athenian Democracy* (Oxford, 1957) is the best account of its subject; R. Barrow, *Athenian Democracy* (London, 1973) is the best bet if a somewhat shorter treatement is wanted.

On the philosophical background, J. Owens, *A History of Ancient Western Philosophy* (New York, 1959) is the best overall account. On Greek ethics and their relevance for politics, C. J. Rowe, *An Introduction to Greek Ethics* (London, 1976) and A. W. H. Adkins, *Merit and Responsibility* (Oxford, 1960) and *From the Many to the One* (London, 1970), are sound guides.

On Greek political thought in general T. A. Sinclair, *History of Greek Political Thought* (London, 1951), D. Kagan, *The Great Dialogue* (New York, 1965) with its companion volume, *Sources of Greek Political Thought* (New York, 1965), C. H. McIlwain, *The Growth of Political Thought in the West from the Greeks to the end of the Middle Ages* (New York, 1932) and L. C. McDonald, *Western Political Theory* (New York, 1968) may profitably be consulted. V. Ehrenberg, *The Greek State* (2nd edn, London, 1969) contains a comparative constitutional study of *polis* government.

D OTHER BOOKS AND ARTICLES MENTIONED

Andrews, P., 'Aristotle, *Politics*, IV, xi, 1296 a, 38–40', *Classical Review* (1952), pp. 141–4.
Barnes, J., Schofield, M. and Sorabji, R., *Articles on Aristotle: I. Science*, (London, 1975).
Cashdollar, S., 'Aristotle's politics of morals', *Journal of the History of Philosophy*, XI, (1973), pp. 145–60.
Cooper, J. R., *Reason and Human Good in Aristotle* (Cambridge, Mass., 1975).
D'Arcy Thompson, Translation of Aristotle's *Historia Animalium* (Oxford, 1910).
D'Arcy Thompson, *Greek Birds* (2nd edn, Oxford, 1936).
D'Arcy Thompson, *Greek Fishes* (Oxford, 1947).
De Laix, R., 'Aristotle's conception of the Spartan Constitution', *Journal of the History of Philosophy*, XI (1973), pp. 21–30.
Diels, H. and Kranz, W., *Die Fragmente der Vorsokratiker* (5th and later edns, Berlin, 1934–54).
Dover, K. G., *Greek Morality in the Time of Plato and Aristotle* (Oxford, 1975).

Düring, I., *Aristotle in the Ancient Biographical Tradition* (Göteborg, 1957).
Ehrenberg, V., *Sophocles and Pericles* (Oxford, 1953).
Finley, M. I. (ed.), *Slavery in Classical Antiquity* (Cambridge and New York, 1968).
Finley, M. I. 'Aristotle and economic analysis', in M. I. Finley (ed.), *Studies in Ancient Society* (London, 1974).
Fränkel, H., *Early Greek Poetry and Philosophy* (Oxford, 1975).
French, A., *The Growth of the Athenian Economy* (London, 1964).
Fuks, A., *The Ancestral Constitution: Four studies in Athenian party politics at the end of the fifth century BC* (London, 1953; repr. Westpoint, Conn., 1971 and 1975).
Guthrie, W. K. C., *In the Beginning* (Cornell, 1957).
Hesiod, *Theogony* and *Works and Days* (trans. D. Wender, Harmondsworth, Penguin Classics, 1973).
Homer, *Iliad* (trans. E. V. Rieu, Harmondsworth, Penguin Classics, 1950).
Hussey, E., *The Pre-Socratics* (London, 1972).
Jaeger, W., *The Theology of the Early Greek Philosophers* (Oxford, 1947).
Kirk, G. S., *The Nature of Greek Myths* (Harmondsworth, Penguin, 1974).
Kirk, G. S. and Raven, J. E., *The Pre-Socratic Philosophers* (Cambridge, 1957).
Kelsen, H., 'The philosophy of Aristotle and the Hellenic-Macedonian policy', *Ethics*, XLVIII (October 1937); reprinted in W. Ebenstein, (ed.), *Political Thought in Perspective* (New York, 1957, pp. 56–86).
McKendrick, P., *The Athenian Aristocracy, 399–31 BC* (Cambridge, Mass., 1969).
Michell, A., *The Economics of Ancient Greece* (2nd edn, New York, 1963).
Morrow, G. R., *Plato's Cretan City* (Princeton, 1960).
Morrow, G. R., 'Aristotle's comments on Plato's *Laws*', in I. Düring and G. E. Owen (eds), *Aristotle and Plato in the Mid-Fourth Century* (Göteborg, 1960), pp. 145–62.
Ostwald, M., *Nomos and the Beginnings of Athenian Democracy* (Oxford, 1969).
Peters, F. E., *Greek Philosophical Terms: An Historical Lexicon* (New York, 1967).
Pohlenz, M., *Freedom and Life in Greek Thought* (Dordrecht, 1966).
Rabinowitz, G., *Aristotle's Protrepticus and the Sources of its Reconstruction* (Los Angeles, 1957).
Rosen, F., 'The political context of Aristotle's categories of justice', *Phronesis*, XX (1975), pp. 228–40.
Ryle, G., *Plato's Progress* (Cambridge, 1966).
Stawell, F. M., translations of Plato's *Apology* and *Crito* in *Socratic Discourses of Plato and Xenophon* (Everyman Library: London, Dent, 1910).
Thomson, G., *Studies in Ancient Greek Society*, Vol. 2 (London, 1955).
Wheelwright, P., *Heracleitus* (Princeton, 1959).
Wieland, W., *Die aristotelische Physik* (2nd edn, Göttingen, 1970).
Untersteiner, M., *The Sophists* (Oxford, 1954).
Ure, P. N., *The Origin of Tyranny* (Cambridge, 1922).
Zürcher, J., *Aristoteles' Werk und Geist* (Paderborn, 1952).

INDEX

Academy, Platonic 15, 99
Achilles 15
Adkins, A. W. H. 26
Aegisthus 21
Aeschines 25
'Aeschylean harmony' 38, 39
Aeschylus 20, 21, 22, 23, 24, 25, 28, 29, 32, 37, 38, 91, 111
Agamemnon 15, 21
Air as origin of life (theory of Anaximenes) 28
akolasia (Aristotle's term for 'incontinence') 84
Alexander the Great 54, 79, 80, 92
Alexandria 55
Anatolia (*or* Asia Minor) 29, 50
Anaxagoras 97
Anaximander 28, 29
Anaximenes 28
Andrews, P. 103
Antigone (Sophocles) 24
Antipater 92, 93
Antiphon 34
Apollo 21, 87
Apology (Plato) 35, 36, 37, 38, 40
Aquinas, St Thomas 82
Arabic civilisation 43
Archilochus 17
Areopagus 20, 21
arete (Classical Greek word for 'excellence', 'virtue', 'know-how') 18, 19, 26, 71
Aristophanes 22, 23, 25, 33
Aristotle: in Dante's Hell 27; 'The Philosopher' for the Middle Ages 27; his expansion of Plato's acceptance of change 35; early biographies of 42; influence of Hippocratic tradition on 42; influence of Platonism on 43; 'Academy phase' and 'exoteric' works of 44; theories in his *Protrepticus* on philosophy, politics and human nature 44–50; 'Wander years' 50–1; influence of his biological studies on his general thinking 51–3; nature and history of the *Corpus* of writings of 53–6; his distinction between wisdom and practical prudence 56; his inclusion of ethics in political science 58; his distinction between theoretical and practical sciences 58; his view of politics as a practical science 59–62; his view of the moral character of politics 59–60; his view of the relativism of politics 61–2; on the role of friendship in politics 62–3; on philosophical contemplation as highest human activity 64; on the family as origin of political community 66; on slavery 67–72; on nature of citizenship and government 72–5; on politics and the common good 76; on types of political regime 76–81; on law and its types 81–3; view that constitutional forms are determined by social composition 86–9; on the 'polity' in theory and practise 89–93; on revolution, its causes and remedies 98–102; his criticism of Plato's political theories 100–1, 104–5; on the soul 107; on happiness, personal and political 106–10; on the ideal state 110–11; on education 110–11; on music 111.
Aristoteleanism 27
Asiatic civilisations 16
Assembly, Homeric 15
Atarneus 51
Athene 16, 21
Athenian Constitution (Aristotle) 77, 87, 91
Athens 15, 18, 19, 20, 21, 22, 23, 24, 33, 36, 37, 38, 43, 50, 51, 54, 55, 69, 71, 73, 80, 81, 83, 87, 90, 91, 92, 93, 98, 101, 106
Attic dramatists 22
Augustine of Hippo, St 109
Augustus 101

Bacchae (Euripides) 25
Bacon, Francis 86
Barker, E. 57, 79, 84, 85, 87, 89, 102, 103, 112